STUDIES ON WOMEN AT MARI

THE JOHNS HOPKINS NEAR EASTERN STUDIES

Hans Goedicke, General Editor

Hans Goedicke, *The Report about the Dispute of a Man with His Ba*

J. J. M. Roberts, *The Earliest Semitic Pantheon*

John D. Schmidt, *Ramesses II: A Chronological Structure for His Reign*

David Lorton, *The Juridical Terminology of International Relations in Egyptian Texts through Dyn. XVIII*

Bernard Frank Batto, *Studies on Women at Mari*

STUDIES ON WOMEN AT MARI

Bernard Frank Batto

THE JOHNS HOPKINS UNIVERSITY PRESS
Baltimore and London

This book has been brought to publication with the generous assistance of the Andrew W. Mellon Foundation.

Manufactured in the United States of America

The Johns Hopkins University Press, Baltimore, Maryland 21218
The Johns Hopkins University Press Ltd., London

Library of Congress Catalog Card Number 73-20696
ISBN 0-8018-1605-X

Library of Congress Cataloging in Publication Data
Batto, Bernard Frank.
Studies on women at Mari.

(The Johns Hopkins Near Eastern studies)
A revision of the author's thesis, Johns Hopkins University.
Bibliography: p.
Includes indexes.
1. Women—Syria—Mari. 2. Women in politics—History. 3. Women in religion—History. I. Title. II. Series: Johns Hopkins University. Near Eastern studies.
HQ1137.S97B37 1974 301.41'2'094781 73-20696
ISBN 0-8018-1605—X

For
Teresa
Rachel, Nathan, and Amos

CONTENTS

LIST OF TABLES

PREFACE

The present book is a revised version of the writer's dissertation which was submitted to The Johns Hopkins University in 1972 in partial fulfillment of the requirements for the degree of Doctor of Philosophy. It is impossible to estimate the contributions of Professors J. J. M. Roberts and Jerrold S. Cooper, under whose direction this dissertation was written.

The writer is also indebted to Professor Herbert B. Huffmon of Drew University, who first introduced him to the study of Akkadian and the Mari texts, for generously making available his extensive files on the Mari personal names. Thanks are also due to Professor Jack M. Sasson of the University of North Carolina at Chapel Hill for a number of helpful suggestions, in particular concerning the letters of Erišti-Aya (ARM X 36-43).

This revised study has profited from the astute criticisms of Professor William L. Moran of Harvard University, who read my dissertation in preparation for publication. Professor Moran's contributions are far more numerous than the credits herein indicate.

Finally, it is a pleasant duty to thank Professor Hans Goedicke for accepting this work into The Johns Hopkins Near Eastern Studies.

LIST OF ABBREVIATIONS

A. Text Sigla for Mari Materials*

A.15	Text published by Dossin, *RA* 42, 128f.
A.455	Unpublished text, tr. by Dossin, "Prophétisme," *Rencontre XIV*, 79-80.
A.1270	Text published by Dossin, *RA* 64, 99-100.
A.2548	Unpublished text, tr. by Dossin, *BARB* 40, 422.
A.2925	Unpublished text, tr. by Dossin, "Prophétisme," *Recontre XIV*, 78.
A.4260	Unpublished text, tr. by Dossin, *ibid.*, 85.
A.4634	Text published by Dossin, *RA* 64, 43.
B 6	Text published by Finet, *AIPHOS* 15, 17-32.
C	Text published by Birot, *RA* 50, 68-72.
"Lods"	Text published by Dossin *apud* A. Lods, "Une tablette inédite de Mari interéssante pour l'historie ancienne du prophétism sémitique," *Studies in Old Testament Prophecy Presented to Professor Theodore H. Robinson*, ed. H. H. Rowley (New York, 1950), 103-10.

B. Bibliographical Abbreviations

ABL	R. F. Harper, *Assyrian and Babylonian Letters* (Chicago, 1892-1914).
ABPh	A. Ungnad, *Altbabylonische Briefe aus dem Museum zu Philadelphia* (Stuttgart, 1920).
AfO	*Archiv für Orientforschung*.

*Quotations from *Archives royales de Mari* (*ARM*/*ARMT*) are cited by volume and number, e.g., VI 23.16 = *ARM* vol. VI, no. 23, line 16. Note, however, that a reference such as Bottéro, *ARMT* VII, 263, refers to the discussion of the editor given on page 263 of the appropriate volume.

AHw	W. von Soden, ed., *Akkadisches Handwörterbuch, Unter Benutzung des lexikalischen Nachlasses von Bruno Meissner (1868-1947)* (Wiesbaden, 1959-).
AIPHOS	*Annuaire de l'Institut de Philologie et d'Histoire Orientales et Slaves.*
ANET	J. B. Pritchard, ed., *Ancient Near Eastern Texts Relating to the Old Testament,* 3rd edition (Princeton, 1969).
ARM	*Archives royales de Mari* (= TCL, 22-) (Paris, 1946-).
ARMT	*Archives royales de Mari* [Texts in transliteration and translation] (Paris, 1950-).
ArOr	*Archiv Orientâlnî.*
AS	Assyriological Studies.
BagM	*Baghdader Mitteilungen.*
BARB	*Bulletin de l'Acadêmie Royale de Belgique. Classe des lettres,* Series 5.
Bezold, *Glossar*	C. Bezold, *Babylonisch-Assyrisches Glossar* (Heidelberg, 1926).
BiOr	*Bibliotheca Orientalis.*
Bottéro, *La femme*	J. Bottéro, "La femme dans l'Asie occidentale ancienne: Mésopotamie et Israël," in P. Grimal (ed.), *Histoire mondiale de la femme. Prêhistoire et antiquitê* (Paris, 1965), vol. 1, 153-247.
BWL	W. G. Lambert, *Babylonian Wisdom Literature* (Oxford, 1959).
CAD	A. L. Oppenheim *et al.*, eds., *The Assyrian Dictionary of the Oriental Institute of the University of Chicago* (Chicago, 1956-).
CAH	*Cambridge Ancient History,* 3rd edition (Cambridge, (1970-).
CH	Codex Hammurapi.
"Cloister"	R. Harris, "The Organization and Administration of the Cloister in Ancient Babylonia," *JESHO* 6, 121-57.
CRAIB	*Comptes rendus... Acadêmie des Inscriptions et Belles Lettres.*
CT	*Cuneiform texts from Babylonian tablets (etc.) in the British Museum.*
Dossin, "Prophêtisme"	G. Dossin, "Sur le prophêtisme à Mari," *Rencontre XIV,* 77-86.
Ellermeier, *Prophetie*	F. Ellermeier, *Prophetie in Mari und Israel* (Herzberg, 1968).
GAG	W. von Soden, *Grundriss der akkadischen Grammatik* (Rome, 1952).
Huffmon *APNM*	H. B. Huffmon, *Amorite Personal Names in the Mari Texts: A Structural and Lexical Study* (Baltimore, 1965).

HUCA	*Hebrew Union College Annual.*
Finet, *L'Accadien*	A. Finet, *L'Accadien des Lettres de Mari* (Brussels, 1956).
Fish, *Letters*	T. Fish, *Letters of the First Babylonian Dynasty* (Manchester, 1936).
JBL	*Journal of Biblical Literature.*
JCS	*Journal of Cuneiform Studies.*
JESHO	*Journal of the Economic and Social History of the Orient.*
JNES	*Journal of Near Eastern Studies.*
KAR	E. Ebeling, *Keilschrifttexte aus Assur religiösen Inhalts,* Band I (= WVDOG 28, Leipzig, 1919).
Kupper, "Baḫdi-Lim"	J.-R. Kupper, "Baḫdi-Lim, préfet du palais de Mari," *BARB* XL, 572-87.
MAM	A. Parrot *et al.*, *Mission archéologique de Mari* (Paris, 1956-).
MSL	B. Landsberger *et al.*, *Materialien zum sumerischen Lexikon* (Rome, 1937-).
"Nadītu"	R. Harris, "The *nadītu*-Woman," in *Studies Presented to A. Leo Oppenheim* (Chicago, 1964), 106-35.
Or	*Orientalia.*
PBS	Publications of the Babylonian Section, University Museum, University of Pennsylvania.
PICO	*Proceedings of the . . . International Congress of Orientalists.*
RA	*Revue d'assyriologie et d'archéologie orientale.*
RB	*Revue biblique.*
Rencontre	*Compte rendu de la . . . Rencontre Assyriologique Internationale.*
Renger *Priestertum*	J. Renger, "Untersuchungen zum Priestertum in der altbabylonischen Zeit," I = *ZA* N.F. 24, 110-88; II = *ZA* N.F. 25, 104-230.
RHA	*Revue Hittite et Asianique.*
RLA	E. Ebeling and B. Meissner, eds., *Reallexikon der Assyriologie (und vorderasiatischen Archäologie)* (Berlin/Leipzig, 1932-).
Römer, *Frauenbriefe*	W. H. Ph. Römer, *Frauenbriefe über Religion, Politik und Privatleben in Mari: Untersuchungen zu G. Dossin, Archives Royales de Mari X (Paris 1967)* (Neukirchen-Vluyn, 1971).
Sasson, "Royal Ladies"	J. Sasson, "Bibliographical Notices on Some Royal Ladies from Mari," *JCS* 25 (1973), 59-78.
SM	A. Parrot, ed., *Studia Mariana* (Documenta et Monumenta orientis antiqui, LV) (Leiden, 1950).

SRT	E. Chiera, *Sumerian Religious Texts* (Upland, Pa., 1924).
TC	*Tablettes Cappadociennes* (1 = TCL 4; 2 = TCL 14; 3 = TCL 19-21).
TCL	Musée de Louvre, Département des Antiquités Orientales, Textes cunéiformes.
UCP	University of California Publications in Semitic Philology.
UET	*Ur Excavations, Texts* (London, 1928-).
UF	*Ugarit-Forschungen.*
VAB	Vorderasiatische Bibliothek.
VAS	Vorderasiatische Schriftdenkmäler der Königlichen Museen zu Berlin.
VT	*Vetus Testamentum.*
VTS	Vetus Testamentum, Supplements.
YOS	Yale Oriental Series, Babylonian Texts.
ZA	*Zeitschrift für Assyriologie und verwandte Gebiete / Zeitschrift für Assyriologie und vorderasiatische Archäologie.*

INTRODUCTION

INTRODUCTION

Interest in the history of woman has never been greater than it is today. Nevertheless it is more by accident than by design that these studies on women at Mari appear at this time. The recent publication of the feminine correspondence from Mari[1] has provided important new materials for an investigation of the role and status of women in the Old Babylonian period. Moderns will perhaps conclude that the women of Mari were subjugated to the male elements of that society according to the familiar and ubiquitous pattern. However viewed from the standpoint of ancient Mesopotamian society, the woman of Mari, like her counterpart in Babylonia, was already much "liberated."

The study of women's role in Mesopotamia has been slighted in the past. The field is not completely barren, of course. Especially noteworthy are the legal studies by A. van Praag[2] and P. Koschaker,[3] the valuable studies on specific classes of women by Landsberger,[4] and Rivkah Harris' prolific writings on the *nadītu*-woman.[5] Bottéro has recently contributed a good, though brief and popular, essay on the woman in ancient Mesopotamia.[6] Nevertheless, a careful, in-depth study of women in ancient Mesopotamia--as for most other social institutions of that culture--has yet to be written.

Since this study was first undertaken some valuable research on the royal ladies of Mari has appeared. Šibtu, the queen of Zimri-Lim, was the subject of a joint study by P. Artzi and A. Malamat.[7] But the most prolific researcher of late has been J. Sasson.[8] We may hope--if the present interest does not wane--that the day will not be long in dawning when a complete social history of the woman not only of Mari but of Mesopotamia in general can be written.

The present study is intended to provide additional building blocks for such a history. The scope of this study is, of course, very narrow, being restricted to the Middle Euphrates kingdom of Mari in the Old Babylonian period, as evidenced by the epigraphic remains preserved from that site. Furthermore, only the role of women in the areas of politics and religion, taking the terms in their widest sense, have been included. (The author hopes, at a future date, to expand his investigation to include other aspects of the role of women at Mari.) The two areas selected for study are, relatively speaking, well documented at Mari. This must not be construed to mean that we possess evidence for the political and religious activities of woman from all levels of Mari society. As might be expected of tablets found for the most part in the royal archives, the majority of these documents deal with persons from the upper echelons of society, and it is primarily with the grand ladies of Mari that we must reckon. Because the texts represent the views of the "aristocracy," the evidence for the lower classes wil be one-sided and distorted. Within these limitations, the role and status of women in the areas of politics and religion can be defined with some degree of accuracy.

The Mari documents of the OB period fall within a very brief span of time. With but a few exceptions, they come from the reigns of the Assyrian subking Yasmaḫ-Addu (1790-1779 B.C.) and the local dynast Zimri-Lim (1779/8-ca. 1745 B.C.).[9] The homogeneity of these texts[10] offers a rare opportunity to reconstruct an accurate picture of the position of woman within that society. Mosaics constructed out of information collected from widely differing locales and times may yield neat and detailed scenes, but their accuracy is necessarily distorted by the juxtaposition of such disparate elements. When an investigator limits himself to evidence drawn from a single period and restricted locale, however, he often pays for this accuracy by a loss of detail. Some areas can be sketched but vaguely because of the paucity of evidence, while other areas must be left completely blank. On the other hand, certain aspects may be overdrawn as a result of the one-sided character of the preserved materials.

Moreover, much of our source material is in the form of letters. Letters are almost always difficult to understand and interpret. Besides the normal philological problems and the cultural gap involved in any translation, the difficulty of translating letters is compounded by not knowing the circumstances which gave birth to the correspondence. Thus the researcher must see beyond the lines in his attempt to reconstruct the background and the situation which governed the relationship between the ancient writer and his correspondent.[11] Occasionally we are fortunate enough to have more than one letter dealing with a single incident. In such cases the chances of correctly interpreting the letter are significantly increased.

Another hazard confronting the modern interpretor is a tendency to confuse the individual with an institution. Letters more often than not reflect the personality and the particular situation of the writer. Without additional evidence, it is difficult to decide whether they also are witness to a universal situation or institution within the culture.

Fully conscious of these and other pitfalls, the author has preferred to sin on the side of conservatism. He has refrained in the main from drawing in extraneous materials in his reconstructions. Likewise, he has declined to speculate on what is not given in the texts, preferring to stress what can be stated positively. This standard has not been a rigid rule, however. The reader will readily observe cases where it has been set aside in favor of a tempting hypothesis. The author believes that by these methods he has presented an accurate, if somewhat circumscribed, picture of women in the areas of politics and religion.

It has already been observed that the position of women in the OB period was far superior to that in the succeeding periods.[12] Boyer[13] and Klima[14] have shown that the legal position of the woman at Mari was not inferior to that of her sister in Babylonia. She possessed equal powers with men before the law in such transactions as adoption, loans, and deposits. In addition, she could contract in her own name and serve as a witness to a contract. She could sue in court or share in an apportionment of goods. She might receive an extensive education and serve as a scribe. She also possessed the power to seal legal and official documents. The following studies will show that this high status of woman at Mari was not confined to the legal realm but extended into other areas as well.

NOTES TO INTRODUCTION

[1]Dossin, *Archives royales de Mari, X: La correspondance féminine* (Paris, 1967).

[2]*Droit matrimonial assyro-babylonien* (Amsterdam, 1945).

[3]Koschaker's writings on women are scattered throughout his works, a list of which may be found in the *Symbolae P. Koschaker*, T. Folkers *et al.*, eds., Studia et Documenta ad Jura Orientis Antiqui Pertinentia, vol. II (Leiden, 1939), 243f.

[4]"Zu den Frauenklassen des Kodex Ḫammurabi," *ZA* 30 (1915-16), 67-73; "Studien zu den Urkunden aus der Zeit des Ninurta-tukul-Aššur," *AfO* 10 (1935), 140-59, esp. 144-49; "Akkadisch-hebräische Wortgleichungen," VTS 16 (1967), 176-204.

[5]See below, chap. 5, n. 1.

[6]*La femme dans l'Asie occidentale ancienne: Mésopotamie et Israël*, in P. Grimal (ed.), *Histoire mondiale de la femme: Préhistoire et antiquité* (Paris, 1965), vol. 1, 145-247.

[7]"The Correspondence of Šibtu, Queen of Mari in *ARM* X," *Orientalia* 40 (1971), 75-89.

[8]See especially his "Biographical Notices on Some Royal Ladies from Mari," *JCS* 25 (1973), 59-78. Other works will be cited at the appropriate places.

[9]Here I follow H. Lewy, "The Chronology of the Mari Texts," *Rencontre XV*, 13-28.

[10]See Huffmon, *APNM*, 8-9.

[11]See the essay of A. L. Oppenheim on the difficulties of translating letters, in *Letters from Mesopotamia* (Chicago, 1967), esp. pp. 54-67.

[12]R. Harris, *JESHO* 9 (1966), 308-9.

[13]*ARMT* VIII, 220-1.

[14]"La vie sociale et économique à Mari," *Rencontre XV*, 45.

PART I

WOMEN IN POLITICS

CHAPTER 1

THE QUEEN AND THE ROYAL HAREM

The Queen

Throughout the long history of Mesopotamia, women have exercised power and influence at the highest political level. According to tradition, in the third millennium the barmaid Ku-Baba was the ruler of Kish,[1] but she is the only ruling queen known to us. On the other hand, several women appear to have wielded considerable influence on the political affairs of their day without holding the title of ruling queen. The reigns of the last two rulers of Lagash in the Early Dynastic Period were notable for the seeming ascendancy of their wives over the polity: the economic records reveal the prominence of Lugalanda's wife Baranamtara and Urukagina's wife Shag-shag, although their prominence may be due in part to the origin of the records, which come from the temples where these women were the chief priestesses.[2] Many centuries later, the Neo-Assyrian queen-mothers Sammuramat and Naqi'a also exercised considerable initiative in the politics of their time.[3] Despite these notable exceptions, little is recorded about the majority of Mesopotamian queens. Consequently, the institution of queenship and the queen's role in Mesopotamian society can barely be sketched even in the broadest of outlines.[4] Until recently documentation for the queenship in the Old Babylonian period has been noticeably lacking. This lacuna can now be partially filled, at least for northern Mesopotamia, with the publication of the feminine correspondence from Mari, and the picture that emerges is surprising both in the wealth of detail that it provides and in the pervasive role of the queen that it reveals. As the following discussion will demonstrate, Šibtu, Zimri-Lim's queen, wielded great influence and in the absence of the king even assumed many of his powers both in domestic and in state affairs.[5]

The identity of Šibtu, as the principal wife of Zimri-Lim, has long been established,[6] thanks to a very important fragment now published as X 119, which describes the inscription of Šibtu's seal: "Šibtu, the daughter of Yarim-Lim, the wife of Zimri-Lim." Šibtu is thus the daughter of the powerful king of Yamḫad, Yarim-Lim. When Zimri-Lim's father Yaḫdun-Lim was killed in a palace revolution and the Assyrians subsequently annexed Mari, the son sought refuge in Aleppo. It was probably during his stay in Aleppo that Zimri-Lim married Yarim-Lim's daughter Šibtu, who returned with him to Mari when Zimri-Lim regained his throne with the help of his father-in-law. Šibtu is nowhere explicitly named as the queen, but both her parentage and her correspondence leaves no doubt that she was the queen. Note especially that the letters from Zimri-Lim addressed to Šibtu by name portray her acting in a manner identical to that found in those letters addressed to or sent by the queen, i.e., *bēltum/bēltija* (X 29;[7] 43; 152-55; 157-64),[8] which are thus also to be ascribed to Šibtu.

After her arrival in Mari, Šibtu maintained contact with her family back in Aleppo. From one letter (X 151) it appears that Šibtu still had enough influence with her father to prevail upon him to look after the interests of one Ḫatni-Addu, apparently one of her favorites.[9] In another instance Šibtu is singled out to receive a portion of the gifts sent to Zimri-Lim from Aleppo by his mother-in-law.[10] Sometime thereafter Ḫammurapi succeeded his father Yarim-Lim as the sovereign of Aleppo. At one point in particular, relations became strained when Šibtu was slandered before her brother. However, after Dadi-Ḫadun conciliated this particular situation,[11] relations between Šibtu and her family probably continued on a harmonious level, as did the official state diplomacy between Mari and Yam-ḫad.[12]

Many other aspects of Šibtu's life are illuminated by the letters. Foremost among these is the joyful announcement of the queen that she had given birth to twins, a boy and a girl (X 26).[13] On several occasions Šibtu sent gifts of clothing to her husband away on a campaign (II 116; X 18; 19). These clothes were perhaps made by the queen's own hand, since on one occasion she explicitly states that she hoped he would proudly wear the garments "which I have made" (X 17.9-13).[14] Like the ideal wife of Proverbs (31: 10-31), Šibtu was all the more dear to her husband because of her industriousness.[15] It is not always clear when the items sent to the king were of the nature of a personal gift. Presumably some of these shipments were part of the rations which Zimri-Lim received as part of regular campaign supplies.[16]

Only occasionally in these state letters is Šibtu's personal affection for her husband revealed, but these rare glimpses attest to her devotion toward Zimri-Lim. Since Zimri-Lim of necessity had to be away from Mari on campaigns much of his reign, recapturing and securing his realm in this era of intrigue and shifting political alliances, one of Šibtu's perennial concerns was for the safety of her husband. To this end she often had omens taken (X 11; 120[17]; 124.18-21[18]). Zimri-Lim, knowing his queen's tendency to anxiety, frequently assured her that he (and the army) was safe and well. One such missive reads:

as-su-ur-ri mi-im-ma ṭe$_4$*-ma-am*
5) *te-še-em-me-*⸢*e*⸣*-ma li-ib-ba-ki*
i-na-aḫ-ḫi-id mi-im-[*m*]*a* LÚ.KÚR *a-na* GIŠ.TUKUL
a-na pa-ni-ia ú-ul ip-ti-na-am
[*š*]*u-*⸢*ul*⸣*-mu-um mi-im-ma li-ib-ba-ki*
[*la i-na*]*-aḫ-ḫi-id*

Perhaps you have heard some rumor and your heart is disturbed--no armed enemy has withstood me! All is well. There is no need to be concerned. (X 123.4-9).[19]

Šibtu naturally looked forward to the day when Zimri-Lim would complete the rout of his enemies and return triumphantly to Mari:

5) *be-lí na-ak-ri-šu*
li-ik-šu-dam-ma
[*i-n*]*a* [*š*]*a-lim-tim ù ḫu-ud li-ib-bi-im*
[*be-lí a-n*]*a ma-ri*[ki] *li-ru-ba-am*

May my lord conquer his enemies. And may my lord enter Mari in safety and happiness (X 17.5-8).

But most of Šibtu's correspondence reveals little about her personality. This impersonal character of her letters can be explained by the official nature of the correspondence that has been preserved.

What Šibtu's letters lack in detail concerning her personal life[20] is more than adequately compensated for by the wealth of detail concerning her duties as queen. It will be shown below that Šibtu wielded broad influence in both domestic and state affairs. This broad influence is demonstrated in her correspondence with Zimri-Lim and with the various high officials of the realm.

For the reader of her letters, the first inkling of Šibtu's personal power comes in the opening sentences to the king. They frequently begin with a report that various places, the palace, the temples, the workshops, and the city, are functioning well. To judge by the most frequent subject of report, Šibtu seems to have been primarily responsible for the direction of the palace: *ekallum šalim* "The palace is fine" (II 116.5; X 6.4; etc.). But other letters show that her responsibility extended to other areas as well, in particular, the temples, the workshops, and even the whole city of Mari: *ekallum šalim bītāt ilāni u neparātum šalmu* "The palace is fine; the temples and workshops are fine" (X 11.4-6; see also 10.3-4); *alum Mari*[ki] *ša*[*lim*] "The city of Mari is fine" (X 23.5; cf. 22.5). These are the reports of an official charged with responsibility for the areas on which he reports[21] (see table 1).

There was some overlapping of jurisdictions, of course, as these same areas were also the responsibility of other officials. Baḫdi-Lim, the prefect of Mari,[22] his successor, Itur-Asdu,[23] and Yasim-Sumu, the *šadubba*,[24] are likewise concerned with the well-being of Mari, the temples, the workshops, and the palace. The lady Addu-duri[25] and Dam-ḫurasi, the secondary wife of Zimri-Lim,[26] also file similar reports for their respective areas of responsibility. Sometimes it is easy to distinguish between the areas of competency of these various officials, as in the case of Dam-ḫurasi.[27] At other times such a distinction is elusive; the boundaries between the authority of various officials were not always clearly delineated.[28] There are other considerations, however, that help to focus the picture somewhat more sharply.

Šibtu's activities do not seem to have been limited to any one area. Zimri-Lim often sends instructions to her to carry out--or to have some subordinate carry out--a specific task. Thus the king instructs Šibtu to summon Ṣidqi-epuḫ, a high-ranking official,[29] and demand of him the bitter garlic that was due from him. Šibtu was directed to personally see to this matter and to supervise the drying and storing of the garlic (X 16 and 136). In another series of letters (X 131-33) the king sends Šibtu instructions concerning the disposition of certain wines, including some for his own use. In this case Šibtu directs the operations of

TABLE 1. REPORTS FROM OFFICIALS ON THEIR AREAS OF RESPONSIBILITY (X *šalim*)

Title	PN	Provincial City	District	Palace	Temples	Work-shops	Palace Personnel	"Girls"	Other
Queen	Šibtu[a]	Mari		X	X	X			
Governor	Baḫdi-Lim[b]	Mari	X	X					
Governor	Itur-Asdu[c]	Mari		X					
Governor	Kibri-Dagan[d]	Terqa	X		(X)[e]				
Governor	Zakira-Ḫammu[f]	Qattunan	X						
Governor	Meptum[g]		X						
šadubba	Yasim-Sumu[h]	Mari		X	X	X			
?	Ibal-El[i]								*nawûm u* DUMU *sim'al*
Commander(?)	Ibal-pi-El[j]								*ṣabum*
King's wife	Dam-ḫurasi[k]						X	X	
?	Addu-duri[l]	Mari		X	X				

[a]See p. 11. [b]VI 15; 18; *et passim.*
[c]*RA* 42, 69; *RA* 66, 116 (A.826):37-38; *ibid*, 119 (A.2801):37-38; see also Dossin, *RA* 42, 125-26.
[d]III 12; 13; 17; *et passim.* [e] *ddagan ù dik-ru-ub*-AN *ša-al-mu*, = the patron deities of Terqa.
[f]II 79-82. [g]*RA* 64, 104; X 155; see below, p. 16. [h]XIII 26; 34;40. [i]II 33; cf. 37.
[j]II 20; *et passim.* [k]See below, p. 22. [l]See below, chap. 3, p. 65.

one Ṣidqi-ṃasi, apparently the cellar-master. When the task is completed, the queen is to hand over certain of the wine to Baḫdi-Lim, the prefect of Mari. These perhaps trivial tasks may conceivably fall within the area of domestic responsibilities. Of more consequence is the role of Šibtu in the dispute between Ḫaya-Sumu and Kiru. The king gives Šibtu instructions to send for Kiru and have her brought back to Mari (X 135).[30] This last example might be taken as a purely familial matter, did it not involve delicate interstate politics which transcend mere matrimonial bonds and familial concerns.

At times Šibtu is clearly the supervisor of lesser administrators and officials. When a crisis developed as the result of illness within the harem, it was to Šibtu that the king wrote, outlining the emergency measures to be taken.[31] Šibtu's supervisory role over the harem is likewise revealed on another occasion. Zimri-Lim, away on a campaign, wrote that he was sending a number of female captives, whom Šibtu was to assign to the textile factories, except for thirty or so of the more beautiful ones who were to be chosen for the king's harem (X 126).[32] This order was later countermanded, but the king continued to rely on the queen to carry out other of his wishes (X 125).[33]

From this last incident it is also evident that the queen was empowered to supervise the activities of the officials Mukannišum and Warad-ilišu. Warad-ilišu was charged with preparing the women who were to enter the king's harem (X 126.16-21). From elsewhere we know that Mukannišum was one of the controllers (X 12.15), a very important group of administrative officials.[34] Warad-ilišu probably belonged to this group also.

The controllers figure prominently in another letter in which the queen's superiority is likewise apparent (X 12). Yaṣṣur-Addu, an official otherwise unknown except in a related fragment (X 13.5), has been sent by the king to show the controllers where certain documents were stored so that they might examine them. But the queen is given the charge to see that the matter is properly conducted. Although the archives has its own superintendent, it is the queen who supervises the investigation and then reseals the door of the archives with her own seal, guaranteeing the integrity of the whole operation. The queen is in this case more than another supervisor; she is the king's personal deputy in a matter of some importance.[35]

Šibtu's sphere of concerns is seen as overlapping with that of the *šadubba* Yasim-Sumu in X 25. In this letter the queen reports the success of one of the king's pet projects, the recently constructed reservoir(?): "On the 24th day (of this month) it rained heavily in Mari. In the middle of the reservoir(?), which my lord built, the water stood 1 'rod' deep."[36] This project was of great personal interest to Zimri-Lim, as evidenced by the attention paid it by Yasim-Sumu (XIII 27-28; 48.4).[37] The project was seemingly under the immediate supervision of Yasim-Sumu. The queen's conduct shows that no area of concern to the king escaped her perusal. The king's interests were in her hands during his absence.

All authority rested ultimately in the king. As did other top officials, the queen normally consulted the king in a variety of cases. Thus Šibtu wrote asking what was to be done in the disposition of the estate of one Bunuma-Addu; the king's answer is contained in X 134.

On the other hand, the queen was widely recognized as personally possessing great influence with the king, so that her intervention was eagerly sought. It is probably in this light that X 160 should be read. The text has been previously treated by Römer, who commented on the multiple problems of interpretation.[39] The letter is a request from Šubnalu to the queen for help in obtaining the release of a certain woman distrained as a pledge (*niputūm*). Ṣidqi-epuḫ has refused to release the woman because she was distrained at the order of the provincial governor (*šāpiṭum*).[40] After explaining the situation, Šubnalu requests the queen to write Ṣidqi-epuḫ instructing him to release the distrainee. Without more information, any exposition of the intricacies of the legal situation involved would be doomed to uncertainty and is perhaps unnecessary for purposes of this study. Both Šubnalu and Ṣidqi-epuḫ were royal officials, the former a controller (X 12.16 and compare 1. 8) and the latter of perhaps somewhat higher rank.[41] But neither of these officials dared act in disregard of the order of the governor. In the opinion of Šubnalu the queen was not so limited, however; she could obtain the release of the distrainee. It is significant that the queen is requested to write directly to Ṣidqi-epuḫ; apparently she need consult neither the king nor the governor. Seldom would even a governor risk acting on his own initiative without consulting the king.[42] It may be going too far to say that the queen had the authority to rescind the governor's order, but it is patent that her word would suffice to counter that of the governor. Probably one must suppose that at Mari the chains of command were to a great extent uninstitutionalized. For this reason it was most important to have someone *mudammiqat awātišu* where it counted the most, namely, with the king.[43] In the case of Šibtu there is no doubt that she wielded great influence with Zimri-Lim, a fact well known to all. Šubnalu's request is thus a powerful tribute to Šibtu's all-pervasive influence.

Another text may confirm Šibtu's preeminence over provincial governors. Tablet X 154 is badly broken and for the most part illegible; for that reason it must be cited with due caution. The letter is addressed to the queen by Itur-Asdu, who at the time of this writing was probably still governor in Naḫur; later he was to become governor in Mari.[44] Itur-Asdu wrote:

> *šum-ma li-ib-bi be-el-ti-ia*
> ÈR *ša-a-tu i-na* É-*ti-ia*
> *li-id-da-ap-pí-ru*
>
> If it pleases my mistress, let them expel (?)[45]
> that slave from my house (lines 5′-7′).

Was the governor here seeking permission for a course of action which lay beyond his competency?

This last incident involving Itur-Asdu may be evidence that Šibtu's sphere of influence was not confined to the palace, the city of Mari, and its immediate environs. Other letters clearly show that her influence extended beyond the territorial limits of Mari itself. In X 153 Kibri-Dagan, the governor of Terqa, writes to the queen, "his mistress," that he will personally see to the case of a certain woman named Partum,[46] about whom the queen had written. Another of the queen's directives involving Terqa is contained in X 27, a letter to Dariš-libur. The queen writes that her instructions regarding the uniform(?) of a youthful servant had previously been disregarded by persons in Terqa. Consequently, she now prevails upon Dariš-libur to expedite the matter since this apparently falls within his jurisdiction.[47]

Letters from other provincial areas likewise point to the queen's power outside of Mari. Ḫali-Ḫadun, who may have been a governor in the Baliḫ region,[48] directs a letter to the queen (X 157). Ḫali-Ḫadun is well aware of the king's presence in nearby (to him) Ašlakka, for the king himself had sent Ḫali-Ḫadun on his present mission (lines 8 f.). Nevertheless Ḫali-Ḫadun sends this progress report of his achievements to the queen. Furthermore, he is even worried that she might think him be less than industrious in his present assignment. It would appear that not only the king but also the queen had to be kept informed of the political developments in the realm. Apparently her opinion was also of considerable importance for advancement in a political career. In a similar manner, Meptum, who seems to be the governor of a district not far from Ešnunna,[49] sends a report of his deployment of troops as well as an intelligence report about the movements of the enemy and their strength (X 155). The end of the letter is illegible; perhaps it would allow us to pinpoint more precisely Šibtu's role in this matter. Nevertheless it is worth noting that Meptum reports on the safety of his district to the queen (line 3), just as he does to the king (*RA* 64, 104.28). Again, Itur-Asdu as the governor of Naḫur (X 152)[50] and Buqaqum, another provincial governor (X 158),[51] send what also seem to be political or military reports; the tablets are badly broken, however, so that no firm conclusions can be drawn. It seems likely that all these reports were sent to the queen because, as in the case of Ḫali-Ḫadun, the king was known to be absent from Mari.[52]

The recognition of the queen's official powers is raised to a new plateau with the revelation that not only Zimri-Lim's own functionaries but even vassal kings paid honor to the queen in terms usually reserved for the suzerain himself. X 159 is a letter from Yasmaḫ-Addu, the king of Yariḫ (a city?, a tribe?).[53] Yasmaḫ-Addu justifies(?) himself for repeatedly sending letters of submission (ÈR-*du-tam*) to the queen, the frequency of which the queen has found annoying. Despite the fact that the rest of the letter is lost, the political implications are manifest. Since Yasmaḫ-Addu regularly wrote to Zimri-Lim (II 53-56), it must be assumed that this letter was addressed to the queen not so much to secure her good graces as to render his acts of allegiance to her in the absence of Zimri-Lim from Mari. This can only mean that Šibtu acted as the quasi-official head of state in place of the king.

The king himself, apparently in recognition of the quasi-independent capacity within which the queen must sometimes operate in his absence, kept Šibtu posted on political developments (X 121.5-17; 122; 132), just as the queen surely kept the king informed of political news that came to her attention.

Somewhat ambiguous is a letter sent to the queen by one Ili-eliš, a man otherwise unattested at Mari. Ili-eliš is obliged to account for his tardiness: "Although they have been paid for in full, the boats have not yet arrived. For this reason I am late. May my lady not be upset."[54] The background of this letter is obscure, but it may be that Ili-eliš was engaged in a royal enterprise and thus owed a report of his mission to the palace, which at this point was being administered by the queen in the king's absence.[55]

A distinction between the powers of the queen and those of the prefect of the palace--or better, governor of Mari--is somewhat elusive, for these two are often seen performing much the same duties. The sphere of both can and does extend beyond the city of Mari into the provinces. However, certain differences are observable. For example, in the supervision of personnel, the queen is primarily concerned with the female personnel of the palace. On the other hand, Baḫdi-Lim is almost exclusively engaged in the deployment of male personnel--the troops, work crews, harvesters, messengers, and the like. But even more characteristic, the normal administration of the district of Mari seems to have been the responsibility of the prefect.[56] The queen's role in administration appears to cover a broader range of activities, cutting across the boundaries of various offices. As has been stated above, the queen enjoyed a certain amount of independence and personal initiative in her own right. But more commonly she seems to have been used by the king as a kind of personal representative who carried out his wishes in extraordinary circumstances. As Birot has pointed out,[57] it is impossible to draw rigid lines between the various offices. Zimri-Lim retained all authority firmly in his own hand and he delegated that authority as he willed. Unlike that of other officials, the queen's jurisdiction was not confined to a specific function. The king relied on her as his principal personal representative or deputy, and consequently, she is observed acting on behalf of the king in many disparate areas.

Šibtu was often engaged in cultic affairs. The regulation of official cultic affairs was part of the king's duty. However, the king frequently entrusted the performance of this duty to the officials in charge of the various regions. Thus Kibri-Dagan, governor of Terqa, wrote that he had carried out the instructions which the king had given concerning the offering of sacrifices to Adad (III 45.15-21). In Mari itself Baḫdi-Lim, prefect of the palace, reports to the king that (in the name of the king) he has ordered the sacrifice to Diritum (VI 74).

Likewise Yasim-Sumu, the *šadubba*, pressed the king to announce the official calendar(?) so that he might establish the date of the sacrifice for Diritum (XIII 29.11-14).[58] It is in an analogous role that Šibtu is observed supervising and administering the cult. Thus on one occasion Zimri-Lim calls upon her to escort the statue of Ḫišametum back to the city Ḫišamta and there offer sacrifice to the goddess:

aš-šu[*m* ^{d}*ḫi-ša-me-*]*tim*
ša S[ISKU]R$_{x}$.RE-*ki*
šu-lu-ki-im
^{m}*ki-ib-ri-*^{d}*da-gan*
iš-pu-ra-am
[*i-*]*na-an-na a-na ḫi-ša-am-ta*
[*a*]*l-ki-ma* ^{d}*ḫi-ša-me*$^{!}$*-tam šu-li-ki*
⌜*ù*⌝ SISKUR$_{x}$.RE *ša-a-tu*
i-qî-i

With regard to conducting Ḫišametum who is (to receive) your sacrifice, Kibri-Dagan has written me. Now then, go to Ḫišamta and conduct Ḫišametum, and offer that sacrifice (X 128).[59]

Šibtu is here performing a task very similar to that performed by the governor Kibri-Dagan in Terqa in honor of the gods Lagamal and Iksudum (XIII 111). Šibtu's active participation in the official cult is also observable in a letter of hers to Zimri-Lim asking whether he would arrive at Mari in time for the sacrifice in honor of Ištar; Zimri-Lim replied in the affirmative (X 120.17-20). The implication appears to have been that if the king would not arrive in time, then Šibtu, as the king's standing representative would herself see to the performance of the sacrifice.[60] However, in another text ascribed by the editor to Šibtu, the queen's close association with cultic matters is confirmed but her hand is inexplicably limited, for she has to ask the king to order some official(s) to give her the sheep that she lacks so that she may offer the customary sacrifice.[61] The intricacies of the bureaucracy at Mari are not always easily set forth. It may be that in this last case the king had previously issued an explicit order which only he was empowered to countermand.[62]

When Šibtu relays to the king various oracular happenings in Mari

(X 6-10), she again functions very much like other officers of the crown, particularly in requiring the symbols of authenticity, the hem and the lock of hair, from the *assinnum* (X 7.23-27). Aḫum the temple administrator brought to Šibtu the oracle along with the hem and the lock of hair from a woman who delivered an ecstatic oracle in his temple (X 8.19-28). One might argue that Aḫum approached Šibtu because he wanted a sure channel to the king for an important oracle. Similarity to parallel situations involving royal officials make it more likely, however, that Aḫum recognized in Šibtu a higher authority through whom he could discharge his own obligation in the affair. It is not out of place to recall again that it was in an official capacity, not just as a concerned wife, that Šibtu sought out the god's will concerning the king's campaigns (X 6.10′-16′; 4.6) and had omens taken for the safety of the king (X 11.8-11; X 120).[63] These same actions were also performed by some of the king's other representatives. The controller Mukannišum had just completed offering sacrifice in the name of the king when he himself witnessed an oracular event which he promptly reported to the king (XIII 23). To some extent Šibtu's cultic role is paralleled, albeit in a lesser capacity, by that of the governor's wife Inibšina[64] and especially by the powerful woman administrator Addu-duri.[65] However, it is the provincial governors who provide perhaps the closest parallel. Baḫdi-Lim, as governor of Mari, commissioned the taking of omens for the safety of the troops and the king (VI 75; cf. 67.7) and accepted in the name of the king the legal symbols of the hem and the lock of hair from a female ecstatic from the temple administrator Aḫum (VI 45). Itur-Asdu, another governor of Mari,[66] also communicated an oracular message to the king and acknowledged that normally he would have required the legal symbols of the prophet in such a case (A.15.50-53). The governor of Terqa, Kibri-Dagan, proceeded similarly in matters involving prophets (XIII 112-14) and also commissioned the taking of omens (III 30.10, 23f.; 41.13-16; 42.10-11; 63.8-9; 84.6, 24).

It may be concluded, then, that in all these matters dealing with the cult--the overseeing and even offering of sacrifice, the commissioning of omen-taking, the supervision of oracular events--Šibtu was acting in her quasi-official capacity as a representative of the king. She could and did perform all the actions the lesser officers did, but she was not limited along jurisdictional lines as were these lesser officers.

Under Zimri-Lim, the queen did indeed play a very important role in the administration of the realm. Her activities extended over many and varying areas. She was often tapped by the king to get some specific task accomplished. One wonders if the king did not actually delegate broad powers to Šibtu in his absence. Caution must be exercised in such speculations, however, as other women, particularly women of the royal family, also played prominent roles under Zimri-Lim. Nevertheless, Šibtu's role is exceptional both in its scope and in the sheer multiplicity of activities in which whe was engaged. Experience must have taught Zimri-Lim that he could rely on Šibtu where ordinary channels were insufficient. This trust, plus her intimacy with the king, made her an extremely powerful woman. Her influence was felt everywhere. It is no wonder that so many curried favor with her.

By way of contrast, her Assyrian counterpart under Yasmaḫ-Addu played virtually no part in the administration of the realm. As in the case of Zimri-Lim, Yasmaḫ-Addu was party to a political marriage negotiated by his father Šamši-Adad and the king of Qatna, Išḫi-Addu.[67] Since the name of Yasmaḫ-Addu's queen remains unknown, it is possible that her correspondence has gone unrecognized.[68] Even so, her correspondence would have to be minimal, since the period is otherwise well-documented, a fact which testifies to the insignificant role Yasmaḫ-Addu's queen must have played in state affairs.

One explanation may be that Yasmaḫ-Addu was not particularly fond of his queen. A fragment, apparently sent by Šamši-Addad to his son Yasmaḫ-Addu, reads:

> Did not the previous kings . . . install their spouse in the palace? Yaḫdun-Lim honored his women-friends but his own wife he put aside, installing her in the desert. Now perhaps you, in the same manner, wish to install in the desert the daughter of Išḫi-Addu. Her father will learn of it and he will be upset. This will not do. There are many rooms in the "palace of palms." Let a room be selected and install her in this room, (but) do not install her in the desert. (A.2548).[69]

Even without knowing the significance of the "desert" referred to here, it is obvious that Yasmaḫ-Addu planned to relegate his wife to an inferior station ill-becoming her dignity. It is reasonable to assume that he did not much care for her. Despised to this extent, his queen could hardly have exerted much influence.

Not to be overlooked is the difference in the reigns of Zimri-Lim and Yasmaḫ-Addu. Zimri-Lim was a powerful, independent sovereign who was forced to spend much time away from his capital city on campaigns subduing rebellious vassals and expanding his frontiers. Yasmaḫ-Addu, on the other hand, was but a provincial vassal king of his father Šamši-Adad and apparently spent very little time away from Mari;[70] he made few decisions independent of his father--and later of his brother Išme-Dagan. In such circumstances Yasmaḫ-Addu's queen would have had little opportunity for independent action in the absence of her husband, even if she were capable of it.

Secondary Wives

In addition to his queen wife, Zimri-Lim undoubtedly possessed a number of secondary wives. This dynast is known to have had at least five palaces; besides the one in his capital Mari, others were located in Terqa, Sagaratum, Dur-Yaḫdun-Lim, and Qattunan.[71] It is likely that the king maintained a harem in each of these residences, at the head of which was probably one of his secondary wives. The situation would thus be analogous to that in the palace in the capital, where, as we have seen, the queen exercised direction over the harem.

Dam-ḫurasi is one such secondary wife of Zimri-Lim. This woman is named on one ration list immediately after Šibtu (VII 206.4.7´) and on another immediately after a list of princesses (C 1.18). The latter text further witnesses to her rank by recording that Dam-ḫurasi, along with one Yatar-Aya listed with her, receives a significantly larger ration of oil than any of the other women, including the king's own daughters and sister. In this ration list the queen unfortunately is not mentioned, depriving us of a comparison of the queen's ration with that of Dam-ḫurasi.

Dam-ḫurasi's importance is also attested in her relatively abundant correspondence (X 62-72). Her letters reveal her to be both beloved by the king and an important lady charged with responsibility over a palace. Despite the fact that much of her correspondence is polite formulae of well-wishing, prayers for the king's victory over his enemies, requests for news, and the like, its very frequency reveals that genuine affection and real concern for the king's safety is involved. In addition, these letters are the quasi-official reports of a woman charged with the supervision of palace personnel and especially the lesser members of the harem. This is their general import: "The palace personnel are well; the girls are well."[72] Thus Bottéro's interpretation of this woman's role in VII 206.10 as the supervisor of certain lesser women of the palace is fully justified.[73] It comes as no surprise, then, when Dam-hurasi takes the initiative in X 72.14-15: ᶠA.ZU *ra-qá-tam ša-ti a-na-ku e-le-qí-ši* "I myself will take (in hand ?) that idle female-physician."

Dam-ḫurasi's high rank is further confirmed by the address of her two letters to the official Sin-muballiṭ, where she styles herself "your mistress" (X 71.4; 72.4). We know little about this Sin-muballiṭ[74] except that he is in the king's entourage and thus can provide information on the king's arrival:

> *i-na-an-na šum-ma ta-ra-ma-ni*
> ⌜*a*⌝-[*l*]*a-ak* LUGAL *an-ni-iš*
> *a*[*n*]*-ni-tam la an-ni-ta*[*m*]
> ⌜*šu*⌝*-up-ra-am*
>
> Now if you love me, send word to me, whether in the affirmative or otherwise, of the king's coming hither (X 71.12-15).

Dam-ḫurasi is anxious to have this information because she must see that the palace is in readiness for the king, should he decide to come.

While it is clear that Dam-ḫurasi is so connected with a palace, it is less patent in which palace she resides. The fact that she appears among those receiving rations from the Mari stores and the fact that her correspondence was found in Mari could be construed as evidence that her palace was that of the capital itself. If this is the case, then Dam-ḫurasi would have exercised a secondary role to the queen Šibtu. A glance at their attested activities shows that the queen's duties and powers far exceeded those of Dam-ḫurasi.

However, a closer inspection of Dam-ḫurasi's letters makes it likely that her palace was the one located in Terqa.[75] X 62 is clearly written from Terqa,[76] for in this letter Dam-ḫurasi requests of her king that he come and kiss the feet of Dagan your lord . . ." (lines 14-16). Dagan "the lord of Terqa"--sometimes in conjunction with the titular god of Mari, Itur-Mer "the king of Mari"--is invoked throughout Dam-ḫurasi's letters as Zimri-Lim's protector and succor (X 62.9f.; 63.15f.; 66.16f.). Such devotion to the god of Terqa may surely be explained by assuming that the writer lives in Terqa and therefore is partially responsible for the official cult in that city, as was her counterpart, Šibtu, in the Mari palace. If the broken tablet X 70 does contain a mention of Dam-ḫurasi's role in commissioning oracles on behalf of her king,[77] then this woman's activities parallel those of the queen even more closely.

On the basis of the foregoing observations, one may suggest that it was something of a standard practice under Zimri-Lim that the chief wife in each of his palaces exercise direction over the female palace personnel and to a lesser extent over the palace itself. Unfortunately we do not know the names of the other wives in comparable positions at the other palaces. With Sasson,[78] it seems justifiable to speculate that Yatar-Aya, named immediately after Dam-ḫurasi and receiving the same generous allotment of oil in C i.19, may have been another such wife of Zimri-Lim.

Some years ago Bottéro had speculated, largely on the basis of the two ration lists we have been considering (Tablette C and VII 206), that Inibšina and Belassunu were also secondary wives of Zimri-Lim.[79] In VII 206.r.8′-9′ these two ladies are listed after Šibtu and Dam-ḫurasi. In C i.20-21 they appear together again, after Dam-ḫurasi and Yatar-Aya, but receive only half the ration of the latter two women, thus suggesting a lower rank. Subsequent publications have confirmed that Belassunu definitely is not a wife of the Mari ruler. Inibšina's status is less clear, but it now appears unlikely that she was a wife of Zimri-Lim either. Our own interpretation of the status of these two women is given elsewhere.[80]

The foregoing reconstruction regarding the secondary wives of Zimri-Lim would be considerably strengthened if similar corroborating evidence were available for Zimri-Lim's predecessors on the Mari throne. We have not been graced with any explicit references to such.[81] Despite the lack of unamibiguous evidence, we may have an attestation of a secondary wife of Yasmaḫ-Addu in the person of Kunšimatum.

Kunšimatum is one of the persons who survived the transfer of power from Yasmaḫ-Addu to Zimri-Lim. Her days under Yasmaḫ-Addu are attested by the single letter X 3, which she wrote to the Assyrian king of Mari. Although the letter is badly broken, enough remains to confirm that she was an important person. All indications point to her permanent residence at Terqa. In Zimri-Lim's time it was the governor of Terqa who wrote informing the king of an illness which struck Kunšimatum (III 63-64). Previously, in her own letter to Yasmaḫ-Addu, Kunšimatum reminded the Assyrian vice-king that she prays for him before Dagan, surely in Terqa. Her position is ambiguous. From her own letter, Kunšimatum appears to have served both a civil and a religious function. Yasmaḫ-Addu reprimanded her for detaining Atta-ili(AN)-ma, a man otherwise unknown (X 3.4-6). After a long broken section, Kunšimatum complained that she has been unjustly slandered (lines 1´-9´) and then continued:

a-na-ku ka-ri-ib-ta-ka I[GI ^{d}]*da-gan*
ú É-*tu ša e-pí-šu ša* [*na-da*]-*ni-im*[82]
am-mi-nim ki-a-am ma-di-iš i-na [*li-*]*ib-bi-ka*
uš-te-ṣú-ni-in-ni eb-bi-ka
šu-ḫi-iz-ma ú bi-it-ka li-ip-qí-du
a-na-ku i-na É-*ti-ka mi-na-am èl-qé*
bu-[*ul-li-iṭ*] *na-pi-iš-ti*
ú-ul ti-de-⸢*e*⸣ [*ki*$^{?}$-*a*$^{?}$]-*am*
an-na-tu-um ša IGI ^{d}*d*[*a-*]*gan*
ak-ta-na-ra-ba-[*k*]*u-um*
um-ma-mi [*ia-ás-m*]*a-aḫ-*^{d}IM
lu ša-li-im-ma
ú a-na-ku i-na ṣí-i[*l-l*]*i-šu*
lu$^{!}$*-ud-mi-iq*

I am the one who prays for you before Dagan. And is the household which I have established to be given away (to another)? Why, then, have they so completely alienated me from your affections? Instruct your controllers that they should inspect your house. What have I taken from your house? Save my life. Do you not

> know that (?!) these[83] are (the words) which
> I constantly pray before Dagan for you: "Let
> all be well with Yasmah-Addu that I for my
> part may prosper under his protection."

According to her own words Kunšimatum exercises some kind of administrative role, managing Yasmaḫ-Addu's "house" in Terqa. It was a position important enough to warrant an audit of the management by the king's controllers. But for this aspect of Kunšimatum's role, one might assign her to the category of priestess and compare her role with that of the *nadītum*-princess, Erišti-Aya,[84] since her insistence upon her role as the king's prayer lady before Dagan implies that Kunšimatum herself considered this to be a major, if not the primary, function in her life. Nevertheless, it is difficult to believe that her words represent anything more than an exaggerated form of the prayers pious persons often recited for their benefactors.[85]

Perhaps one is justified in speculating that, like Dam-ḫurasi with Zimri-Lim, Kunšimatum was a (secondary) wife of Yasmaḫ-Addu. In that case both her administrative role over the king's "house" as well as her frequent prayers for her lord (and husband?) would be paralleled later in the person of Dam-ḫurasi, Zimri-Lim's secondary wife in the same city.[86] When Zimri-Lim regained the throne of his fathers by ousting the Assyrian ruler, Kunšimatum would have become part of the victor's spoils. As in Israel, the new king acquired the harem of the former king as part of legitimizing his claim to the throne. This would explain the concern of Kibri-Dagan, Zimri-Lim's governor in Terqa, when this woman became gravely ill. The governor had omens taken and they were favorable; whereupon he wrote assurances to the king not to worry.[87] Further documentation, however, will be necessary to confirm this hypothesis. Should Kunšimatum indeed be Yasmaḫ-Addu's (secondary) wife, then we could unhesitatingly posit a quasi-institutionalized role for the secondary wives in the Mari kingdom whereby they assumed some positive direction over the palace and female personnel.

Lesser Women of the Harem

Undoubtedly there were many women at Mari who belong within the group which may be designated as the lesser women of the harem.[88] Their types and numbers are difficult to ascertain, however. The harem may be referred to in VII 206.8, where the proposed restoration [. . .*sé-e*]*k-re-tum* "women of the harem" has much merit; nevertheless, certainty is excluded here.[89] Indeed one may speculate with justification that this tablet is a ration list for the whole of the royal harem, including the female servants and domestics. Palace domestics should be included within the designation "women of the harem," as in the Middle Assyrian practice.[90] Proof of this may be found in VIII 88, a document which apparently records the sworn testimony of "12 women of the palace" that they belonged to the royal harem.[91] The lesser members of the harem as a group were usually referred to under the ambiguous sumerogram SAL.TUR.(MEŠ), which may stand either for *ṣeḫḫertum* "a young girl"[92] or, especially in the plural, for *ṣuḫārātum* "girls"--a specific class of women.[93] The girls who belong to this class had the honor of being attached to the palace and supported by it. Some of these girls belonged to the royal harem,[94] but others did not.[95] Those girls who belonged to Zimri-Lim's harem were under the direction of the king's chief wife in the palace.[96]

The origin of these harem women is interesting. While some may have derived from local stock (they may have been the daughters of local functionaries),[97] many seem to have been of foreign origins, particularly prisoners of war. In a series of letters concerning the assignment of new female captives, we learn that the majority were assigned to the royal textile factories as weavers. But a few exceptionally perfect female captives were selected for the royal harem, as the following two letters demonstrate:

a-na ^f^*ši-ib-tu*
qí-bí-ma
[*u*]*m-ma be-el-ki-ma*
[*a-n*]*u-um-ma* ^f^UŠ.BAR.MEŠ *uš-ta-ri-ki-im*
[*i-n*]*a li-ib-bi-ši-na* NIN.DINGIR.RA.MEŠ
[*i-b*]*a-aš-še-e* NIN.DINGIR.RA.MEŠ *bi-ri-ma*
a-na É ^f^UŠ.BAR.MEŠ *pi-iq-di-ši-na-ti*
i-na ^f^UŠ.BAR.MEŠ *an-ni-tim*
ú i-na ^f^UŠ.BAR.MEŠ *pa!-ni-tim*[98]
i-na li-ib-bi-ši-na
30 ^f^UŠ.BAR.MEŠ *ú-lu-ma ma-li*
ša na-sa-qí-im dam-qa-tim

a-di ⸢*ša*⸣*-ar-tim ša qa-qa-di-im*
šu-um-ma-na-am la i-ša-a ús-qí-ma
a-na ÈR-*ì-lí-šu pi-iq-di*
ù ÈR-*ì-lí-šu ši-it-ra-am šu-ba-re-em*
[*l*]*i-ša-ḫi-is-sí-na-ti ù ti-im-mi-nu-ši-na*
[*l*]*u nu-uk-ku-ru-ú a-na* ŠUK-*ši-na*
nu-uḫ-ḫi-di-ma zi-mu-ši-na
la i-na-ak-ki-r[*u*]
ù i-nu-ma ^{f}UŠ.BAR.M[EŠ]
ta-na-as-sà-qí ER[-*ì-lí-šu*
li-i[*ṣ-ṣu-ur-ši-na-ti*(?)]
ù mu-ka-ni-ša-am [*nu-uḫ-ḫi-di-ma*]
zi-im ^{f}UŠ.BAR.MEŠ *ša-n*[*e-t*]*im*
ša ta-pa-aq-qí-di-šum
la i-na-ak-k[*i-ir*]

To Šibtu say, thus (says) your lord: I have just sent you some female-weavers. In among them are (some) *ugbabātum* priestesses. Pick out the *ugbabātum* priestesses and assign them (i.e., the rest) to the house of female-weavers. From among these female-weavers and from the previous female-weavers choose from them 30 female-weavers--or however many who are choice (and) attractive, who from (their) toenail(s) to the hair of (their) head(s) have no blemish(?)--and assign them to Warad-ilišu. And Warad-ilišu is to give them the Subarean veil (?). Also their status-document(?)[99] is to be changed. Give instructions about their rations, so that their appearance does not worsen. And when you select the female-weavers, let Warad-ilišu guard(?) them.[100] Also instruct Mukannišum that the appearance of those other female-weavers whom you assign to him is not to worsen (X 126).[101]

According to this first letter, Zimri-Lim would have his queen, in his absence, select the women who were to enter his harem. But in a subsequent letter (X 125) Zimri-Lim writes that he has changed his mind and that he personally will select his "girls for the veil" (SAL.TUR.MEŠ *ši-it-ri-im*)[102] from the female captives at hand. Apparently Zimri-Lim did not relish the idea of anyone else choosing which women were to be in his harem!

The personal attention that Zimri-Lim gave to his harem is vividly illustrated also in another incident. Reacting to a rumor that the woman Nanname was sick, Zimri-Lim rushes stern instructions to his queen in Mari that the rest of the women of the harem are to be protected. No one is to use her drinking cup, chair, or bed. She is to be quarantined and kept in isolation. It is better for the one woman to die than that the whole harem become sick, for the woman's illness is contagious (X 129-130).[103] X 14 contains the queen's reply; she has carefully carried out the king's instructions.

The women threatened by illness in the preceding incident are obviously the women of Zimri-Lim's harem, for the sick woman "is residing much (of the time) with the palace-personnel" (X 129.6-7).[104] This in itself would be enough to prove that the women the king is worried about are his harem. But in addition there is a reference to the lesser women of the harem that has hitherto gone undetected. MÍ.MEŠ *ma*-DA-*tim* (line 8)--whether to be read *sinnišātim mâdātim* "many women" or "the lesser women" (*s. maṭâtim*)--refers to the members of the harem other than the king's wives, as in the Middle Assyrian royal edict: *lu-ú aššāt*$^{meš\text{-}at}$ *šarri lu-ú sinnišāti*^{meš} *ma*-DA-*a-tu* "either the wives of the king or the lesser/many women (of the harem)."[105]

It may be concluded from these letters that the king's wife did not live in the same quarters as the rest of the harem. That the queen had her own quarters is proven by the mention of the "house of the queen" (*bīt bēltim*) in XIII 26.9.[106] Presumably a secondary wife also had separate quarters in her respective palace and had little contact with the lower members of the harem. The lesser women of the harem, on the other hand, would appear to have lived together in common quarters. They shared vessels, chairs, beds, etc., hence the injunction that the other women were not to use the sick woman's cup, chair, or bed (X 129.10-16; 14.6´-7´) and that she should be given separate, isolated quarters (*bītum parsum*, X 130.4; 14.6´).

Conclusion

The queen at Mari under the vassal kingship of Yasmaḫ-Addu seemingly played a comparatively insignificant role in public affairs. Under the independent Zimri-Lim, by way of contrast, the queen (*bēltum*) was an extremely influential woman in both domestic and state affairs. Her role was especially evident in the king's absences from Mari, the queen often acting as Zimri-Lim's personal deputy above and beyond the normal institutional lines of jurisdiction.

The king had other wives who resided in his provincial palaces. Under Zimri-Lim, at least, these secondary wives supervised the lesser members of the royal harem and perhaps exercised other administrative functions as well in their respective palaces. Little is known of the lesser members of the harem (variously designated as *ṣuḫaratum* or as *sinnišātum maṭâtum*) except that they were of various origins, including war captives, and that they lived together, sharing common quarters.

NOTES TO CHAPTER 1

THE QUEEN AND THE ROYAL HAREM

[1]Jacobsen, *Sumerian King List*, AS 11 (Chicago, 1939), 104, v 35-42; Bottéro, *La femme*, 211.

[2]See M. Lambert, "Les Dieux-vivants à l'aube des temps historiques," *Sumer* 5 (1949), 8-33; C. J. Gadd, *CAH*³ 1/2, 120; Y. Rosengarten, "La civilisation sumérienne de Lagash," *Revue philosophique de la France et de l'étranger* 155 (1965), 407f. Although no queen, Enḫeduanna, the daughter of Sargon of Akkad and high priestess of the moongod Nanna of Ur, may have exercised a somewhat analogous role; for the life of Enḫeduanna, see Hallo and van Dijk, *The Exaltation of Inanna* (New Haven, 1968), 1-11.

[3]See Meissner, *Babylonien und Assyrien* (Heidelberg, 1920), I, 74f.; Donner, "Art und Herkunft des Amtes der Königinmutter im Alten Testament," *Festschrift Johannes Friedrich* (Heidelberg, 1959), 105-45, esp. 110f.; Bottéro, *La femme*, 212f.; Oppenheim, *Ancient Mesopotamia* (Chicago, 1964), 104. The monograph of H. Goossens on Semiramis, cited by Oppenheim, *Ancient Mesopotamia*, 359, n. 34, was apparently never published; but now see W. Eilers, *Semiramis: Entstehung und Nachhall einer altorientalischen Sage* (Vienna, 1971).

[4]See Landsberger, "Akkadisch-hebräische Wortgleichungen," VTS 16 (Leiden, 1967), 198-204.

[5]This writer reached his conclusions independently of Artzi and Malamat, "The Correspondence of Šibtu, Queen of Mari in *ARM* X," *Or* 40 (1971), 75-89, and thus was pleased to find their position in substantial agreement with that espoused in this study.

[6]Dossin, "Šibtu, reine de Mari," *PICO* XXI (1948), 142f.

[7]Sasson, "Royal Ladies," 76, thinks it "inconceivable" that letter X 29 was dictated by Šibtu, the queen, Elsewhere *bēltum* is patently the title of the queen; compare, for example, a letter written by the princess Erišti-Aya "to the queen, my mother" (*a-na be-el-tum um-mi-*[*ia*], X 43.1), where this woman is explicitly called the wife of the king: "I am a king's daughter; you are a king's wife" (DUMU.MÍ LU[GAL *a-na-ku*] / *aš-ša-a*[*t* LUGAL] / *at-ti*, ll. 12-14). For this reason it seems unwise to exclude from the queen's dossier a tablet whose fragmentary state precludes a clear understanding of its contents.

[8]It is uncertain whether the letters written by the woman bearing the title *bēlet mātim* (II 117; X 20; 28) should be ascribed to the queen or to another person. Missing from her letters to Zimri-Lim is the phrase *amatka(-ma)* "your servant," which is normal in Šibtu's letters to Zimri-Lim. Artzi and Malamat, *Or* 40 (1971), 77-79, speculate that *bēlet mātim* may have been the title of the queen-mother. If *bēlet mātim* is the queen-mother, one may compare her role in Ugarit, Israel, and the Neo-Assyrian period; see Donner, "Art und Herkunft des Amtes der Königinmutter im Alten Testament," *Festschrift Johannes Friedrich*, 105-45. Letter X 20 has been treated by M. Powell, Jr., "A Note on the 'imērum' Measure at Mari," *RA* 67 (1973), 77-78.

[9]This difficult letter has been treated by Römer, *Frauenbriefe*, 80-82, and, somewhat inaccurately, by Artzi and Malamat, *Or* 40 (1971), 86-88.

[10]X 30.12. The sender of this letter, *ka-še-rum*, is surely the same person whose name is elsewhere written *ga-še-ra*, the wife of Yarim-Lim, mother-in-law of Zimri-Lim; see Dossin, *RA* 64 (1970), 98, n. 4, and 102. Gašera is the recipient of a gift of tin from Zimri-Lim in letter A.1270.13; see *ibid.* Additional information about Gašera is contained in X 139 and VII 237.7′; see Sasson, "Royal Ladies," 74.

[11]X 156; for a summary of this letter and the (uncertain) identity of Dadi-Ḫadun, see Artzi and Malamat, *Or* 40 (1971), 89.

[12]On the relations between Mari and Yamḫad, see Dossin, *RA* 36 (1939), 46-50; *BARB* 38 (1952), 229-239. For a somewhat different view, see Sasson, *BiOr* 28 (1971), 356.

[13]For this letter, see Artzi and Malamat, *Or* 40 (1971), 81.

[14]For this letter, see *ibid.*, 82; in line 12f. read *ana bu-di-šu* (not *idi-šu*) *liškun*. See also chap. 5, n. 48, below.

[15]One is also reminded, although less directly, of the description Ludingira gives of his mother in the first "sign" by which she may be recognized; see Civil, "The 'Message of Lú-dingir-ra to His Mother' and a Group of Akkado-Hittite 'Proverbs,'" *JNES* 23 (1964), 1-11, esp. p. 3, ll. 10-20; Cooper "New Cuneiform Parallels to the Song of Songs," *JBL* 90 (1971), 158.

[16]If *bēlet mātim* is the queen (see above, n. 8), then Šibtu also sent various kinds of flour and legumes to her husband (X 20) and once asked to be excused for not being able to send any presents at the moment (II 117).

[17]See Römer, *Frauenbriefe*, 37, n. 2.

[18]For the relevant sections of X 11 and X 124, see Artzi and Malamat, *Or* 40 (1971), 82; in X 11.15-17 read: *ittum šakin ša pī ilim bēlī lipuš* "The sign is certain (lit., established), let my lord do the command of the god."

[19]See further Zimri-Lim's reports on his safety in X 121.18; 124.24; 127.7.

[20]Whether the Šibtu of VIII 76.3 who loans money to one Sin-iqišam is to be identified with the queen remains in doubt; see Boyer, *ARMT* VIII, 112, n. 1.

[21]See Birot, "Les lettres de Iasim-Sumu," *Syria* 41 (1964), 27-28; Marzal, "The Provincial Governor at Mari: His Title and Appointment," *JNES* 30 (1971), 200.

[22]See Kupper, "Baḫdi-Lim," 573.

[23]B.58.26-7, *RA* 42, 69; Dossin, *RA* 66, 116 (A.826.37-38) and 119 (A.2801.37-38); see further Dossin, *RA* 42, 125-26.

[24]See Birot, *Syria* 41 (1964), 27-28.

[25]See below, chap. 3, p. 65.

[26]See below, pp. 21-23.

[27]*Ibid.*

[28]Birot, *Syria* 41 (1964), 63-64.

[29]See below, pp. 14-15, and n. 41.

[30]See below, chap. 2, p. 48.

[31]See below, p. 28.

[32]See below, pp. 26-28.

[33]See below, p. 27, and chap. 4, pp. 83-84.

[34]On the *ebbū*, see Moran, "New Evidence from Mari on the History of Prophecy," *Biblica* 50 (1969), 30, and references cited there. On Mukannišum, see below, chap. 4, p. 85, with n. 28.

[35]For a similar incident in which the king employes Inibšina, see below, chap. 3, p. 60. Both incidents with the relevant texts (X 12; 82; XIII 14) have been studied by Sasson, "Some Comments on Archive Keeping at Mari," *Iraq* 34 (1972), 55-67. See also comments by Artzi and Malamat, *Or* 40 (1971), 83.

[36]This letter has been treated by Dossin *apud* Birot, *Syria* 41 (1964), 34; Römer, *Frauenbriefe*, 92-93; and by Artzi and Malamat, *Or* 40 (1971), 85, who correctly read the verb *izzizūnim* in l. 14.

[37]See Birot, *Syria* 41 (1964), 34-35.

[38]This letter has been translated in part by Artzi and Malamat, *Or* 40 (1971) 84.

[39]*Frauenbriefe*, 75-77.

[40]On *šāpiṭum* as a title for a provincial governor at Mari, see Marzal, *JNES* 30 (1971), 186-217.

[41]On Šubnalu, see Sasson, *Iraq* 34 (1972), 60-61. Ṣidqi-epuḫ's official capacity is unknown. In X 160 he seems to be of higher rank than Šubnalu, in that Šubnalu wrote first to him for permission to release the pledge. On the other hand, Ṣidqi-epuḫ's authority in the matter may stem from his special competency in agricultural matters; see above, p. 11, and possibly IX 6.5,7,12; 34.6; XII 57.6. See also X 138.8′; VI 39.24, 25; and Birot, *ARMT* IX, 330.

[42]See Kupper, "Correspondance de Kibri-Dagan," *Syria* 41 (1964), 116.

[43]The writer gratefully acknowledges Moran (private communication) as the author of this idea.

[44]On Itur-Asdu, see below, chap. 2, p. 39, with n.6, and pp. 40-41.

[45]Although *liddappirū* is by form apparently II/2 and therefore expected passive, the presence of the accusative *wardam šâtu* seems to require an active meaning.

[46]It seems highly unlikely that this woman was a weaver, as Römer's (*Frauenbriefe* 69) restoration [*ú*]*š*!? *-pa-ar-tim* suggests. The correct reading is surely ⸢f⸣*pa-ar-tim*.

[47]On this letter, see Finet, "Le ṣuḫārum à Mari," *Rencontre XVIII*, 69. The item in question (TÚG.BUR.KÀL) is apparently a garment; Finet would make it the uniform of the *ṣuḫārum*, "emblème de sa function"; similarly Marzal, "Two Officials Assisting the Provincial Governor at Mari," *Or* 41 (1972), 366. Römer (*Frauenbriefe*, 68) suggests the reading TÚG.NÌ.-BÀRA "eine Art Matratze."

[48]Finet, *ARMT* XV, 144. See Birot, *RA* 66 (1972), 138, who translates ll. 8-16 of X 157.

[49]See Dossin, *RA* 64 (1970), 106.

[50]X 152 has previously been published by Bottéro, *RA* 52 (1958), 173-76.

[51]Finet, *ARMT* XV, 153, Puqâqum.

[52]One should also include X 165, for which the address is lost, among the queen's correspondence. In this letter the anonymous writer, on assignment in the north country informs his "mistress," the queen, that he has carried out the king's instructions regarding the countries Kurda, Andariq, and Karana. He adds that he is about to return to Andariq, where he will effect the setting up of the king's throne, i.e., Zimri-Lim's suzerainty over that country; when he has completed that mission he will send another report to the queen.

[53]On Yasmaḫ-Addu, see Birot, *ARMT* IX, 251-2; Rowton, "Urban Autonomy in a Nomadic Environment," *JNES* 32 (1973), 213.

[54]*i-ša-ri-iš ap-la ú* GIŠ.MÁ<.MEŠ> *a-di-ni ú-ul ik-šu-da aš-šum ke-em uḫ-ḫu-ra-ku li<-ib>-bi be-el-ti-ia la i-na-ḫi-id* (X 161.6-11). Römer's (*Frauenbriefe*, 92) forced reading of lines 6-7, *i-ša-ri-iš ap-la-ku*!? "Korrekt bin ich(!) befriedigt worden" is not necessary.

[55]Should *bēlet mātim* turn out to be the queen (see above, n. 8), letter X 28 would also be relevant here. In this letter *bēlet mātim* scolds Yassi-Dagan for not sending anything for the support of his son Ḫaya-abum and takes the opportunity to suggest a gift for herself as well; see Finet, "Le ṣuḫarum à Mari," *Rencontre XVIII*, 69. Yassi-Dagan, a highly placed official under Zimri-Lim, was himself the son of La'um, another well-known official from the Assyrian period; see Birot, *ARMT* IX, 328 and 356; Huffmon, *APNM*, 43; and XII 141.4.

[56]See Kupper, "Baḫdi-Lim," for a discussion of the prefect's powers.

[57]*Syria* 41 (1964), 64.

[58]*Ibid.*, 27-28. See further below, chap. 3, pp. 67-68.

[59]This incident is elsewhere mentioned in a text cited by Dossin, "Le panthéon de Mari," *SM*, 48: 1 *ku-li-lum kaspum* 10 *šiqlu* KI.LÁ.BI *a-na* d*ḫi-ša-m*[*i*]*-tim sa ḫi-ša-am-ta*^{ki} *i-na a-la-ki-ša* "1 silver wreath weighing 10 shekels for Ḫišametum of Ḫišamta at the time of her journey."

[60]An analogous situation may well lie behind 142.25-31, in which Zimri-Lim instructs Addu-duri about his pending arrival and all that she is to prepare for the sacrifice in honor of Diritum. On Addu-duri and the similarity of her role to that of Sibtu, see below, chap. 3, pp. 64-72, esp. 67f.

[61]X 15. This text is not completely legible; after a break the text reads: 13)*be-lí ša ṭà-*⌜*ra*⌝*-di- im* 14)[*l*]*i-iṭ-*[*ru*?*-da*]*m*?*-ma* 15)*lu-ul-*[*li*]*k*?*-ma* 16)SISKUR$_x$.RE [*š*]*a-a-ti* 17)*lu*'*-uq-qi* ⌜*ù*⌝ *be-lí* 18)*li-wa-*⌜*e-er*⌝*-ma* 19)UDU.ḪI.A *a-na* SISKUR$_x$.RE 20)*ki-ma ša-na-as-su-um-ma* 21)*li-*⌜*id*⌝*-di-nu-nim* 22)UDU.ḪI.A *ú-ul i-šu* "let my lord send what is to be sent so that I may go(?) and offer that sacrifice. And let my lord order that they give me sheep for the sacrifice just as (they have) up to the present year. I have no sheep!" On *šanassuma*, see Kraus, "'*ūmšum*' und Verwandtes," *RA* 62 (1968), 77-79. It should be noted, however, that the address of this letter is partially lost so that it is not absolutely certain that Šibtu is the author.

[62]Baḫdi-Lim, the prefect of Mari, likewise had to seek decisions from the king in certain matters involving the authority of several lesser

officials within their own areas of competency; see VI 39; 40.

63 See above, p. 10.

64 See below, chap. 3, pp. 60-61.

65 See below, chap. 3, pp. 65-69.

66 See Moran, *ANET*³ 623.

67 See below, chap. 2, p. 52.

68 Sasson has suggested that Akatiya of X 171 and 178 may have been one of the wives of Yasmaḫ-Addu (*BiOr* 28 [1971], 354). If this is correct, then the Assyrian queen received political reports from the king (X 178) and a lesser official (X 171 and perhaps 172) similar to those received by Šibtu. However, the identity of Akatiya is not certain. She may be identical with the woman by the same name mentioned in a text from the time of Zimri-Lim, who, to judge from other names in the text, seems to be a ruler of a provincial town (VII 217.3). This Akatiya is to be distinguished from the woman of that name mentioned in C iii.8.

69 Published in translation only by Dossin, *BARB* 40 (1954), 422.

70 See, for example, I 69.

71 Bottéro, *ARMT* VII, p. 229.

72 É.GAL-*lum ša-lim* SAL.TUR.MEŠ *ša-al-ma*, X 63.6f.; 64.6f.; 66.6f.; 67.6f; 68.6f.; cf. 65.6, where reference to *ekallum* is omitted. On the meaning of *ekallum*, see below, n. 104. On the official character of these reports, see above, p. 11.

73 *ARMT* VII, 99 and 238f.

74 This official is not to be identified with the person of that name in VII 180.iii.7′ (a *ba'ir* from Urbat) or IX 24.ii.18 = 27.ii.37 (a *re'u*). Sasson, "Royal Ladies," 59-60, thinks that X 71.9 "apparently considers him to be a brother, real or political, of the king." If this is correct, then we have here important confirmation of Dam-ḫurasi's eminent position.

75 So also Sasson, "Royal Ladies," 59-60.

76 So also Moran, *Biblica* 50 (1969), 55.

77 See Römer, *Frauenbriefe*, 60; Sasson, "Royal Ladies," 60.

78 Sasson, "Royal Ladies," 60.

79 *ARMT* VII, 240f.; *La femme*, 191f., 210.

80 See below, chap. 3.

81 There is possibly a reference to Yasmaḫ-Addu's harem in the sarcastic rebuke of Šamši-Adad to his son:*a-ḫu-ka an-ni-ki-a-am da-am*$_x$*-da-am i-du-uk ù at-ta aš-ra-nu-um i-na bi-ri-it* SAL.MEŠ *ṣa-al-la-at* "Your brother (Išme-Dagan) has defeated (the enemy) here, while you lie there idling among the women!" (I 69.8′-11′). However, the point of this remark is not so much that Yasmaḫ-Addu is frolicking among his harem; rather it is a reference to the indolent and cowardly character of the Mari ruler. This interpretation is strengthened by the following admonition, "When you go forth with the army to Qatna, be a man (*lu-ú a-wi-la-at*)!" (1. 13′). In this study of women, it is not out of place

to note the import of this disparaging statement for the native cultural evaluation of women, namely, that they are weak and unheroic.

82 I owe the restoration of this line to Moran.

83 *an-na-tu-um* = F. pl. of *annû* "this." At Mari the plural is normally *anni'atum* > *annêtum; annâtu(m)* is the normal later form (see *GAG* #45, a).

84 See below, chap. 5, pp. 96-98.

85 See below, chap. 10, pp. 129-32.

86 See above, pp. 21-23.

87 [f*ku-u*]*n-ši-ma-tum* [*im-ra-aṣ*]*-ma* [*ap-ta-la*]*-aḫ te-re-tim a-na šu-ul-mi-ša ú-še-pí-iš-ma te-re-tum ša-al-ma li-ib-bi be-lí-ia mi-im-ma la i-na-ḫi-id* "Kunšimatum has become ill and I was concerned (about her condition). I have had omens taken for her health and the omens are favorable. May my lord not worry" (III 63.4-12), following the restorations of von Soden, *Or* 21 (1952), 85. See also III 64, with corrections by Falkenstein, *BiOr* 11 (1954), 117; see further Finet, "Les médecins au royaume de Mari," *AIPHOS* 14 (1954-57), 126-27.

88 On the analogous Middle Assyrian category, see Weidner, "Hof- und Harems-Erlasse assyrischer Könige," *AfO* 17 (1956), 262.

89 See the discussion of Bottéro, *ARMT* VII, 239. Cf. the widespread use of the designation *sikrētum* in the Neo-Assyrian period; Landsberger, VTS 16, 201.

90 See Weidner, *AfO* 17 (1956), 262.

91 See Boyer, *ARMT* VIII, 241.

92 III 8.6; X 124.4; 140.16; 114.5, etc.; see further chap. 6, p. 108, with n. 2, below.

93 See Birot, *ARMT* IX, 342; Finet, "Le ṣuḫārum à Mari," *Rencontre XVIII*, 65-72.

94 See Birot, *ARMT* IX, 342, and Römer, *Frauenbriefe*, 73.

95 The woman Aḫatum described as a SAL.TUR in IX 24.iii.28 is surely the same as the woman by that name in X 8.6, where her full identity is given: mf*a-ḫa-tum* SAL.TUR d*da-gan-ma-lik* "Aḫatum, the 'girl' of Dagan-malik." This girl could hardly belong to the royal harem, since her master is specifically given as Dagan-malik.

96 See above, pp. 11-17, and 22-23.

97 See Birot, *ARMT* IX, 342.

98 Römer, *Frauenbriefe*, 70: *an!né-tim.*

99 See Römer, *Frauenbriefe*, 71, n. 5. If *temenum* does refer to a document, then it surely refers to the tablet in which the captives were assigned their new status or role in captivity; see X 123.16. The status of these women is to be changed from that of female-weaver to that of "girl of the Subarean veil."

100 There is insufficient evidence for postulating that the Mari harem was attended by eunuchs, as in the Middle Assyrian court and afterward. On the probability that Warad-ilišu was a controller, see above, p. 13.

[101]Cf. Römer, *Frauenbriefe*, 70-71, who reads differently in details.

[102]For text X 125, see below, chap. 4, pp. 83-84. Other references to women wearing the veil (*šitrum*) at Mari are contained in X 137.10′, XIII 22.41, 45. See further, below, chap. 2, p. 39. Instead of "veil," Sasson, *BiOr* 28 (1971), 356, suggests "singing" (*šiṭrum*) without, however, proving his case.

[103]X 129 has been translated by Finet, *AIPHOS* 14 (1954-57), 129 and treated also by Artzi and Malamat, *Or* 40 (1971), 85. Römer, *Frauenbriefe*, 57-58, transliterates and translates X 129 and gives a summary of X 130.

[104]*ù it-ti* É.GAL-*lim ma-ga-al wa-aš-ba-at-ma*. For *ekallum* in this meaning, see Weidner, *AfO* 17 (1956), 262f.; *AHw* 192 *ekallu(m)* A 2a.

[105]See Weidner, *AfO* 17 (1956), 262: "Der Ausdruck *sinnišâti mâṭâti* 'niedere Frauen,' der einmal begegnet (Z. 56) scheint alle Frauen zu bezeichnen, die einen geringeren Rang als die Gattinnen des Konigs einnehmen."

[106]A similar conclusion has been reached by the excavator on the basis of archaeological data; see Parrot, *Le Palais: Architecture, MAM* II/1, chap. 7, esp. 177f.

CHAPTER 2

THE KINGS' DAUGHTERS

The Mari documents provide considerable information about the lives, as well as the position, of the princesses of Mari, especially the daughters of Zimri-Lim. Inibšina and Erišti-Aja are treated elsewhere.[1] In this section the roles of Inib-šarri, Kiru, Šibatum, and Tizpatum will be examined in detail. Other princesses will be considered as the evidence permits.

Inib-šarri

The case of Inib-šarri is intriguing in its elusiveness. It is very difficult to trace the career and activities of this woman. That she was the daughter of Zimri-Lim is clear. In one of the economic tablets, she is among the nine women receiving oil rations who are designated as "daughters of the king" (DUMU.MÍ.MEŠ LUGAL, C i.7). Her letters leave no doubt that her royal father was Zimri-Lim.

At the time the above-mentioned oil rations were distributed, Inib-šarri may have been residing in Mari. The rest of her attested activities, however, seem to have taken place outside of Mari, in Naḫur and Ašlakka, located in the territory (*mātu*) known as Yapturum (XIII 144.3-4, 30f.). Her miserable residence in Ašlakka and Naḫur is the constant theme of her letters (*ARM* II 112-13; X 73-79). Unfortunately, many of the implications of these letters escape us because of a lack of knowledge of their background. Attempting to reconstruct the situation implied by her correspondence, I suggest the following hypothesis. At the time of his capture of Ašlakka, Zimri-Lim confirmed Ibal-Addu on the throne of Ašlakka as his vassal.[2] At the same time a marriage was arranged between Ibal-Addu and Zimri-Lim's daughter Inib-šarri--against her will--in order to strengthen the bond between the suzerain and his vassal. Zimri-Lim had good reason to suspect, as subsequent events were to confirm, that Ibal-Addu would never be a docile vassal. Ibal-Addu already had a wife, but Inib-šarri was supposed to become the principal wife and the queen of the city. Nevertheless, once Zimri-Lim departed from the area, Ibal-Addu proceeded to act rather independently. He spurned Inib-šarri, restoring his first wife to her former preeminent position. Such a hypothesis would give sense to the following complaint of Inib-šarri to her father:

aš-šum mu-ru-u[ṣ l]i-ib-bi-ia
1-*šu* 2-*šu a*[-*na ṣe*]-*er be-lí-ia*
aš-pu-ra-am-ma b[*e-l*]*í ki-a-am*
iš-pu-ra-am um-ma-[*a-*]*mi al-ki*
a-na áš-la-ak-ka-a^{ki} *er-bi-ma*
la ta-ba-[x x]*-a-ki be-lí an-ni-tam*
iš-pu-ra-am [*i-n*]*a-an-na a-na áš-*[*l*]*a-ka-a*^{ki}
e-ru-ub-ma mu-ru-uṣ li-ib-⌜*bi*⌝*-im*
ma-di-iš a-na-aṭ-ṭà-al
^{f}*aš-ša-at i-ba-al-*^{d}IM
ši-ma šar-ra-at ù MU.D[U]
a-lim^{ki} *áš-la-ka-a*^{ki} *ù a-la-*⌜*né-e*⌝
MÍ *ši-ma im-ta-na-aḫ-ḫa-ar*
ù i-ia-ti i-na ṭú-ub-qí-im
ú-še-ši-ba-an-ni-ma
ki-ma ^{f}*le-el-la-tim*
i-na qa-ti-ia li-ti-i
uš-ta-aṣ-bi-ta-an-n[*i-ma*]

Concerning my unhappiness I have written twice to my lord, and my lord wrote me (a reply) as follows: "Go and enter Ašlakka. Do not ..."[3] This is what my lord wrote me. Now I have entered Aslakka, but I am very unhappy. The wife of Ibal-Addu--she is the queen! And that woman herself constantly receives the gifts[4] from (both) Ašlakka and the (other) cities, while she (he?) makes me sit in a corner and grasp my cheek in my hand like some female-simpleton! (X 74.4-21).

The foregoing passage does not state explicitly that Inib-šarri was married to Ibal-Addu. Nevertheless, there are other indications which also suggest this conclusion. In X 75.5 reference is made to a *terḫatum* which was brought to the king[5] apparently as part of the arrangements for the marriage of Inib-šarri. What is surprising is that Inib-šarri is already in the vicinity of, if not actually in, Ašlakka. This is evident from the reference in this letter to Itur-Asdu, the governor of Naḫur,[6] an important figure in this controversy between Inib-šarri and Ibal-Addu. Perhaps the marriage was hastily arranged, and a promise made that the *terḫatum* would be paid later--a promise which is now being fulfilled.

A remark made by Zimri-Lim to his daughter to cover her head may offer additional evidence of her status as a married woman. In reply to his daughter's request to be allowed to return to Mari, Zimri-Lim tells her, *al-ki* É-*ki šu-ta-aṣ-bi-ti-ma šum-ma ú-ul ri-it-tum qa-qa-ad-ki ku-ut-mi-ma at-la-ki-im* "Go and manage your household.[7] But if it is not possible(?), then cover your head and come away to me." (II 113.4-6; similarly X 76.5-9). Veiling of the head by the married women of ancient Mesopotamia is a custom which is attested but as yet ill defined.[8] This would be the earliest reference to this practice. And while the phrase *qaqqadam katāmu* in this connection is not otherwise attested,[9] the equivalent *qaqqadam paṣānu* is used in the Middle Assyrian Laws.[10] Furthermore, *katāmu* is attested in phrases referring to the veiling of a bride.[11] If this injunction to veil her head is a reference to Inib-šarri's married status, then it is to be assumed that no divorce had taken place, if one was contemplated. However, caution must be exercised in claiming that Zimri-Lim's admonition to his daughter to cover her head implies a married status. If this assumption is made, it is difficult to see how the alternatives could be either to stay with her husband or else to veil herself. Perhaps Zimri-Lim's statement should be interpreted to mean, "If you cannot manage your own household, then cover your head and depart (in shame)."

Whatever the nature of her relationship with Ibal-Addu, it is clear that Inib-šarri considered herself mistreated by the king of Ašlakka. In addition to being spurned and relegated to an inferior position (X 74.13-21, Inib-šarri complains that she has been placed under heavy guard (X 74.26-27). In another letter she insists that, since leaving her father's house, she has been without sufficient food or firewood (II

113.20-23). In short, she is quite miserable in her present situation (X 74.29-30; II 113.23-24).

Perhaps the motive behind Ibal-Addu's ill-treatment of Inib-šarri was an attempt to reassert his political independence. He seems to have been scheming with the Eluḫutians for some manner of revolt:

i-na pa-ni-tim-ma ki-ma i-ba-al-^{d}IM
a-lam ša-ni-im-ma pa-ni-šu
iš-ku-nu a-na [*be-l*]*í-ia aš-pu-ra-am*
i-na-an-na a-wa-tu-šu
i[*k-t*]*u-na it-ti i-lu-ḫu-ta-yi*
[ ]-*am*
(Break)
Rev. [*i*]*a*(?)
[ ] x x x [x]-*ni*
ù *ṭe*$_4$*-ma-am ma-li a-ta-ma-ru*
a-na be-lí-ia lu-ud-bu-ub
ú-la-šu-ma LÚ *šu-ú*
i-na-ak-ki-ir-ma
ki-ma bu-zu-ḫu-um i-ba-aš-ši
ú-ba-az-za-ḫa-an-ni
ù *ṭe*$_4$*-ma-am an-ni-im* 1-*šu* 2-[*šu*]
⌜*a-na*⌝ *i-túr-ás-du aš-pu-ur*

Previously, when Ibal-Addu decided to go to another city, I wrote to my lord. Now his words have been confirmed. With the Eluḫutians.... Let me relate to my lord a report of all that I have been observing. If not, that man will rebel and he will oppress me in whatever manner possible (lit. according to the oppression there is present). Now this report I have twice sent to Itur-Asdu (X 77.4-10´).

It was perhaps not long after that we find Inib-šarri in Naḫur, as evidenced by letters II 112-113 and X 76.[13] She seems to have fled there, seeking the protection of Itur-Asdu, the governor of Naḫur. Itur-Asdu evidently had jurisdiction over neighboring Ašlakka. His authority, however, was somewhat limited. At least Ibal-Addu felt sufficiently independent to ignore the directives issued by the governor:

ù i-túr-ás-du ik-šu-dam-ma
2-šu 3-šu aš-šu-mi-ia
a-na i-ba-al-^{d}IM *iš-pu-ur-ma*
da-ḫa-at a-wa-ti-šu i-ba-al-^{d}IM
ú-ul i-ša-al

And Itur-Asdu came here and wrote to Ibal-Addu three times concerning me. But Ibal-Addu has ignored his instructions (II. 113.32-36).

Zimri-Lim sent instructions to his daughter--and implicitly to Ibal-Addu as well--that she should return to Ašlakka and her husband.[14] Inib-šarri's objections to this counsel proved correct. Ibal-Addu did not bring her back to Ašlakka at all; he left her confined in Naḫur.[15] Inib-šarri's pleas to be allowed to return to Mari were to no avail at this time as the roads were unsafe, for in a subsequent(?) letter she is still entreating:

a-di ma-ti i-na na-ḫu-ur^{ki}
wa-aš-ba-k[u]
sa-li-mu-um it-ta-aš-ka-an
ù KASKAL *i-te-še-er*
be-lí li-iš-pu-ra-am-ma
li-it-ru-ni-in-ni
ù zi-im be-lí-ia
ša ú-za-mu-ú
lu-mur

How long am I to stay in Naḫur! Peace has been established and the roads are safe. Let my lord write that they should bring me back so that I may look upon my lord's countenance of which I am (presently) deprived (II 112.5-13).

Letters relating the outcome of Inib-šarri's adventures are not preserved. Whatever the reality of Inib-šarri's hypothesized marriage to Ibal-Addu, she could expect some income (MU.DU "gift") from certain cities in the region, one of which was Ašlakka (X 74.14-16). Naḫur apparently was another, for she had quarters(?) there (II 113.18-19; X 76.14-16). Part of Inib-šarri's income (MU.DU) ended up in the coffers of Mari, intended no doubt to maintain--or secure--her good standing with the powers that be.[16] Along with other rulers of provincial towns, Inib-šarri is listed among those who have sent gifts (MU.DU) to Mari (VII 125; 203.1; IX 241.9-10). Her appearance among such company raises new possibilities. We suspect that, as in the case of Kiru in Ilanṣura, Inib-šarri held an office in addition to her possible role as queen.[17]

Kiru and Šibatum

We turn our attention now to another daughter of Zimri-Lim who was certainly invested with political authority as a duly appointed public official. We are speaking of Kiru. Once again the preserved documents leave great lacunae in our knowledge of this princess, even while providing considerable information. Kiru was Zimri-Lim's daughter. In C i.10 she is listed as one of the *mārāt šarrim* receiving oil rations from the palace stores. And from her own correspondence it is clear that her royal father is Zimri-Lim: she addresses him as *abī* "my father" and identifies herself as *māratka* "your daughter" (X 31-35, address; note also [*a-b*]*i ù be-lí* 31.8ʹ and *a-bi* 31.18ʹ).

The early part of Kiru's career is hidden from us. Most, if not all, of her correspondence dates from approximately the same period. At this period she was residing in Ilanṣura in the country of Idamaraz.[18] From her letters we surmise that she was the wife and queen of Ḫaya-Sumu, the ruler of Ilanṣura.[19] She apparently was also the mayor of that city, as will be shown momentarily.

Zimri-Lim had, evidently, given his daughter in marriage to Ḫaya-Sumu in another of his political moves to strengthen his control over that part of his realm. Ḫaya-Sumu, like Ibal-Addu and other local rulers in the north country, was ambivalent in his allegiance to Zimri-Lim, a reality Zimri-Lim was well aware of.[20] The marriage between Kiru and Ḫaya-Sumu, however, was far from being harmonious. Numerous difficulties presented themselves, and eventually, it seems, the marriage was dissolved.

Fortunately, there is explicit documentation for Kiru's marriage to Ḫaya-Sumu; even in the moment of declaring his intention to be rid of Kiru, Ḫaya-Sumu acknowledged that she is his wife (*aššatum*, X 33.28). In another letter Kiru reminds her father that it was he who caused her present misery by arranging this marriage: *a-bi ù be-lí a-na* GIŠ.GU.ZA ᶠ*šar-ra-tim* ⌜*ú*⌝-*še-ši-ba-an-ni* "My father and lord (himself) installed me on (this) queen's throne!" (X 34.8ʹ-10ʹ).

Such a marriage of expediency no doubt produced tensions of its own. Nevertheless, part of the strained relationship between Kiru and her husband stemmed from a conflict in authority--the product of another of Zimri-Lim's unusual moves. Not only did he give Kiru to Ḫaya-Sumu to be his wife and queen; he also gave her authority in her own right by appointing her as the mayor (*ḫazannum*) of Ḫaya-Sumu's city-state. In the midst of one of their disagreements, Ḫaya-Sumu reportedly threatened to kill Kiru:

> *it-bi-ma ḫa-ià-sú-ú-mu-um pa-ni-ia*
> *um-m[a-m]i ḫa-za-nu-ta-am an-ni-nu-um*
> *wa-aš-ba-ti iš-t[u] a-na-ku úš-ma-at-⌜ki⌝*
> *li-li-kam-ma ka-ka-ab-ki!*
> *li-te-er-ki-i ...*
>
> Ḫaya-Sumu arose and (spoke) thus to my face, "You exercise the mayorship[21] here.[22] (But) since I will (surely) kill you, let him come--your star--and take you back!" (X 32.11′-15′).

We do not know the circumstances which provoked this violent outburst, but we may fairly suppose that the duality of Kiru's role was involved. Ḫaya-Sumu apparently felt that his wife looked more to her father's interests than his own. This is, of course, what Zimri-Lim had counted on.

We cannot pass on without a comment on Kiru's distinctive position as mayor. As a woman mayor, Kiru is unique in the whole of cuneiform literature. Precisely because of this uniqueness, one might question the accuracy of a statement spoken in a moment of violent rage.[23] Nevertheless, there are no indications in these documents that Ḫaya-Sumu has exaggerated Kiru's functions. Indeed, there is supporting evidence for Kiru's mayoralty. In another letter from which the address is lost but which may confidently be assigned to Kiru on the basis of internal evidence,[24] Kiru is revealed as capable of assuming responsibility for the direction of Ilanṣura:

> *a-na-ku-ú ù at-ti pu-ḫu-ur-ma*
> *ni-la-ak ù a-la-am*
> *a-na ma-an-ni-im ni-iz-zi-ib*
> *a-di a-na-ku iš-tu ma-ri*^{ki}
> *a-tu-ur-ra-am an-ni-ke-em-ma*
> *ši-bi*

> Should you and I both go together (to Mari)? To whom would we entrust the city? (Rather) stay here until I return from Mari (and then you can go) (X 113.6-11).

We believe that these words refer less to Kiru's role as wife and queen of the ruler of Ilanṣura than to her responsibility as the mayor of the city. Ḫaya-Sumu implies that if both he, the king, and Kiru, the mayor, are absent at the same time, the city would be left without any responsible authority.

Other of Kiru's activities have less certain connection with her role as mayor and may derive simply from the considerable influence she enjoyed with other leaders of the region as daughter of the Mari monarch. Thus Zu-ḫatni[25] brings his message of political import to Kiru rather than some other official, for example, Ḫaya-Sumu. Whether Kiru is acting in some official capacity or simply as an intermediary in forwarding a message to Zimri-Lim is impossible to say. Kiru's prestige is further attested by her prevailing upon one Yarim-Dagan, the ruler of Dunnum,[26] to act as her intermediary and intercessor before Zimri-Lim (X 33.10f.; 35.5f.). Of doubtful significance for Kiru's legal status is X 35 in which Kiru informs Zimri-Lim that a lion is responsible for the deaths of Zimri-ḫammu and two women.[27]

On another occasion we find Kiru offering advice on matters political. In X 31 she pointedly reminds her father that it was to his detriment that in the past he had ignored her counsel concerning the Ḫanaeans. She warns him not to spurn her counsel a second time, even though she is only a woman.[28] (Note the cultural implication concerning the lowly status of women!) Not only did Kiru believe herself to be an astute assayer of political events of the day, but she apparently even felt that her words had the authority of the gods themselves. Nevertheless, her father's reluctance to follow her advice may indicate a different assessment of the worth of Kiru's opinions.[29]

Not all of Kiru's difficulties can be attributed to a conflict of loyalties. A second factor which strained relations between Kiru and her husband was the rivalry of another woman, Šibatum.[30] This woman was a constant thorn in the side of Kiru, who opens one of her letters (X 33) with the lament:

ik-ta-ru na-ba-aš-ti
i-na ši-tá-am-mi a-wa-at ^{f}*ši-ba-tum*

My patience has worn thin at listening over and over to Šibatum's complaints! (11. 5-6; cf. 17-18).

Kiru continues with a plea that she be allowed to return to her native city, elaborating the impossibility of her present situation in Ilanṣura. Her husband has disgraced her in the presence of other kings and then added injury to insult by taking away from her a certain woman (slave) and giving her to Šibatum. Probably from this same disagreement stems still another letter in which Kiru decrys her ill-treatment in Ilanṣura and Šibatum appears in the role of adversary. Šibatum insolently taunts Kiru with her own (Šibatum's) readiness to accept Zimri-Lim's will, while Kiru is solely preoccupied with returning to Mari, even against her father's wishes (X 32.20′f.). The beneficiary of Kiru's misfortunes in Ilanṣura, Šibatum could smugly proclaim her satisfaction with the present arrangement.

But who is this Šibatum? Our documentation is incomplete, and Šibatum's prosopography can only be surmised from vague references, often in broken contexts. Apparently Šibatum is also a daughter of Zimri-Lim, perhaps by an inferior wife, who somehow followed her half(?)-sister Kiru to Ilanṣura. Sasson has offered the tempting suggestion that Zimri-Lim had given two daughters in marriage to the ruler of Ilanṣura and that Šibatum was the one favored by both her father and her husband.[31] This hypothesis cannot be maintained in its entirety, however. There can be no doubt that Kiru, at least theoretically, was the superior of the two women. In addition to being the mayor of the city, she was also Ḫaya-Sumu's wife (*aššatum*; X 33.28) and queen (X 34.8′-10′). Comparable statements concerning Šibatum are lacking. Indeed, the only information we have concerning the legal status of Šibatum is contained in her enigmatic remark to Zimri-Lim:

at-ta-a-ma a-na TUR.SAL-*tim*
ù a-na DUMU.UŠ *ta-ad-di-na-an-ni*

You yourself gave me into daughtership and son-/heirship[32] (X 95.5-6).[33]

We can only assume from this statement that Zimri-Lim is Šibatum's father, possessed of legal authority to "give" up his daughter. However, this terse statement is filled with difficulties of interpretation. Is this a case of adoption, as normally implied in the expression *ana mārtūtim nadānum*? If so, to whom was Šibatum given for adoption? What is the implication of the compound phrase, to be given "into daughtership and son-/heirship"? The addition of "son-/heirship" would seem to imply a privileged position beyond mere "daughtership." Was a marriage with certain (unusual) legal conditions involved?[34] A matrimonial adoption? Given the context of Kiru's and Šibatum's rivalry and Ḫaya-Sumu's favoritism toward the latter at the expense of the former, we perhaps must assume, as does Sasson, that both women were married to Ḫaya-Sumu. However, since the letter continues with a complaint about how Kiru has deprived Šibatum of a certain gardner (l. 6f.), it would appear that the two women were not on an equal legal footing. Šibatum thus finds it necessary to appeal to her father for redress in restoring certain legal rights guaranteed her at the time of her marriage. Kiru has exceeded her powers and wronged Šibatum, while the latter is completely innocent:

> [*a-na-ku*] *ù* ᶠ*ki-r*[*u-ú*]
> [*n*]*i-iš* DINGIR.MEŠ *ni-iz-*[*ku-ur*]
> *mi-im-ma ḫi-ṭì-tum ù g*[*u-ul-lu-ul-tum*]
> *it-ti-ia ú-ul i-ba-aš-ši*
>
> Kiru and I have sworn an oath. There is neither fault nor guilt on my part (ll. 3´-6´).

We speculate that Šibatum was indeed a daughter of Zimri-Lim given in marriage to Ḫaya-Sumu, along with Kiru. However, as she was of inferior status to Kiru, Šibatum was given an improved legal standing by making her an adoptive daughter with full rights of inheritance.

Šibatum ends her letter with a request for a lapis lazuli cylinder seal inscribed with her name so that her missives will be accepted as authentic (ll. 7´-12´). In II 115.15-17 Šibatum reiterates her request for a cylinder seal.

We have previously referred to Kiru's accusations against Šibatum. Šibatum was not idle in protecting her own reputation against these and similar accusations. "Why," she wrote Zimri-Lim, "are they forever slandering me before my lord? They are continually accusing (me) of untrue things to my lord!" (II 115.9-14).[35]

Other of Šibatum's activities are normal enough for a princess. In another letter (X 94)[36] there is perhaps a reference to her early career; but little can be gleaned from the broken lines. The reverse of the tablet concerns a dream, the veracity of which Šibatum is anxious to have verified by Zimri-Lim. Sasson has plausibly demonstrated that X 5 is also from Šibatum, not Šibtu.[37] In this letter the writer reports on political developments in her region, to which Ḫaya-Sumu is party. She concludes with a sigh of relief at the news that Zimri-Lim is well, adding a bit of flattery in an allusion to Zimri-Lim as her mainstay:

> . . . *a-na* [*ma*]-*ma-an*
> [*a-na-a*]*ṭ-ṭà-al ú-ul a-na k*[*a-t*]*a-a-ma*
> [*a-na-a*]*ṭ-ṭà-al*
> [*at-t*]*a-a-ma a-bu-um ù* SES-*ma*
> *a-ia-ši-im*
>
> Shall I look to someone? Is it not to you alone that I look? You are both father and brother to me! (X 5.37-41).

Šibatum's letters prove that she was not powerless. Indeed, she must have been either a likable woman or a crafty one who thoroughly ingratiated herself with her husband and to a lesser extent with her father--at the expense of her rival Kiru.

Kiru's situation did not improve. On the contrary, relations between herself and her husband disintegrated so completely that the marriage was eventually dissolved. A letter previously mentioned, in which Kiru pleads with her father for permission to return to her native city, records the widening rift:

> [x x]x *a-ia-ši lu ba-al-ṭà-ta*
> [*i-na ba-t*]*i-iq-ti-ni*
> [*m*]*a-ḫa-ar* LUGAL.MEŠ
> [*i*]*b-tu-uq um'-ma šu-ma*
> *at-la-ki a-na* É *a-bi-ki*
> *iš-tu pa-ni a-ša-ti-ia*
> *a-mu-*⌈*ur*⌉
>
> ...may you keep well for my sake. In our (mutual) accusation he denounced (me) before the kings in the following terms: "Go away to your father's house! I have looked away (in disfavor) from the

face of my wife!"[38] (X 33.23-29).

Because of the fragmentary condition of the letter, it is impossible to determine whether this incident occurred within an assembly of kings convoked to arbitrate the dispute or, more likely, in a garrulous moment in the presence of other local rulers. Kiru felt herself--and her father's house--so thoroughly disgraced by the incident that a continuation of the marriage was absolutely impossible.

Ḫaya-Sumu does not appear to have been dissatisfied with the way matters were developing; he, too, seemingly desired the dissolution of the marriage. From a letter of Zimri-Lim to Šibtu (X 135), we learn that in negotiations concerning Kiru, Ḫaya-Sumu has requested that Zimri-Lim send for Kiru and bring her back to Mari. Zimri-Lim, himself away from the capital, instructs his queen to comply with Ḫaya-Sumu's request and have Kiru returned to Mari.

Since no further information is available, we do not know whether this marriage ended in a formal divorce. Nevertheless, we are left with the impression that the rupture was irreparable. Presumably also, Šibatum remained in Ilansura, content with her lot.

Tizpatum

Another daughter of Zimri-Lim is Tizpatum. Our knowledge of this woman is practically limited to one letter.[40] Because of its importance, that letter is given here in its entirety.[41]

a-na be-lí-ia
qí-bí-ma
um-ma ^{f}*ti-iz-pa-tum*
GÉME-*ka-a-*[*m*]*a šum-ma i-na ki*<-*na*>-*a-tim*
be-lí a-lam$_{x}$ *šu-na-a*^{ki} *i-ra-am*
ù ^{m}*i-lí-*IŠDAR ÈR-*šú*
1 ME *ṣa-*[*b*]*a-am ù* 1 ÈR-*ka ták-lam*$_{x}$
ar-ḫi-⸢*iš*⸣ ⸢*ṭu*⸣*-ur-dam-ma*!
a-al-ka ù ÈR-*ka šu-zi-ib*
ú-la-šu-ma a-lam$_{x}$ KÚR *i-ṣa-ab-ba-as-sú*
i-na-an-na aš-šum-mi-ia-ma
LÚ *ṣa-ar-mu-šu*! *um-ma-a-mi*
ki-i DUMU.MÍ *zi-im-ri-li-im*
a-ḫi-iz ù ú-zu-un-šu

15) *a-na ṣe-er* ^m^*zi-im-ri-li-im*
ša-ak-na-at a-na an-ni-tim
a-bi ù be-lí li-iṣ-ri-im

To my lord, say, thus (says) Tizpatum your servant: If in truth my lord loves the city[42] Šuna and Ili-Ištar is his servant, then quickly send one hundred troops and some trustworthy[43] servant of yours and save your city and your servant. Otherwise the enemy will seize the city. Now, precisely on my account are people concerned about him, saying, "How can he be married to the daughter of Zimri-Lim and be loyal to Zimri-Lim!"[44] Let my father and lord take note of this (X 98).

Ili-Ištar is the ruler of Šuna; elsewhere he is called "the ruler (lit., man) of Šuna.[45] His is obviously the person who in lines 13f. is married to the daughter of Zimri-Lim, i.e., Tizpatum. This was another of those politically motivated marriages arranged by the Mari dynast. Šuna was located in the turbulent north country, perhaps not far from Ašnakkum, one of the city-states characterized as ready to oppose Zimri-Lim.[46] Ili-Ištar was thus vulnerable to ambitious, hostile neighbors. In the instance outlined here, Šuna was faced with an impending attack. In terms of the overall international picture, the threat must have appeared rather insignificant to Zimri-Lim secure in remote Mari, especially if a mere one hundred troops would be sufficient to stave off the threat. Accordingly, he ignored the request from his vassal for aid. But to the inhabitants of Šuna the threat was all too real, hence the urgency of Tizpatum's pleading. She hoped to move her father where her husband had failed. To prod her father to quick action, Tizpatum reminds her father that others in the area--friend and foe are eyeing the fate of Šuna. If Zimri-Lim is unwilling or unable to respond vigorously in the case of a city whose ruler is both a loyal vassal and son-in-law of Zimri-Lim, is he likely to come to the defense of other cities in the region! To default in this situation would be an open invitation to further attacks and even rebellion.

There is no evidence for assuming that Tizpatum held any office or acted in any official capacity. Rather, her letter is that of a daughter hoping to succeed when the official channels had failed. This would be evidence of the importance of having an influential voice in the right place. Incidentally, this letter does confirm that political marriages were expected to produce firm alliances and ready cooperation between the parties so allied.

Other Daughters of Zimri-Lim

TABLE 2. DAUGHTERS OF ZIMRI-LIM*

Name	Residence	Status	Husband
Inib-šarri	Alaškka	queen	Ibal-Addu
Kiru	Ilanṣura	queen/mayor	Ḫaya-Sumu
Šibatum	Ilanṣura	wife(?)	Ḫaya-Sumu
Tizpatum	Šuna	wife, queen(?)	Ili-Ištar
Erišti-Aya	Sippar	*nadītum*	
Ibbatum	Andariq	wife, queen (?)	Ḫimdiya
Naramtum	?	queen(?)	?
Duḫsatum	?	?	?
Kiḫila	?	?	?
Aḫatum	?	?	?
Ḫazala	?	?	?

*This list may not be exhaustive; see below, n. 47, and chap. 5, n. 61.

In addition to Inib-šarri, Kiru, Šibatum, Tizpatum, and Erišti-Aya, Zimri-Lim had other daughters. Ibbatum, Duḫšatum, Kiḫila, Aḫatum, Ḫazala, and Naramtum are all designated as *mārāt šarrim* in C i.6-13. Only for Inibšina the *ugbabtum*, who heads the list in C i (ll. 4-5), is there any evidence that she may be the daughter of a king other than Zimri-Lim.[47] Presumably, then, the others are all daughters of Zimri-Lim.[48]

Ibbatum (C i.6) is surely identical with Inbatum, the writer of letters X 84-86. Sasson[49] has gathered together practically everything that is known about this princess. She was married to Ḫimdiya, a vassal king of Andariq who succeded (deposed ?) Atamrum in that position. In her sole significant letter (X 84),[50] Inbatum is defending her husband's actions to a suspicious and angry Zimri-Lim. Ḫimdiya's intent was in no way inimical in capturing the rebellious city of Amas. Ḫimdiya, she insists, remains a loyal vassal of her father. Here once again is underscored the importance of having someone *mudammiqat awātišu* before the king. Inbatum's personal circumstances are not disclosed in the preserved documents.

Naramtum wrote three letters (X 44-46). Unfortunately, little is revealed about the author's situation except that she is unhappy in her provincial residence. Naramtum complains to her father that even the slave girls of her own palace despise her because they see that she is ignored back in her father's house. She protests that she ill deserves such treatment and asks for redress (X 46.4′f.). One other text records that Naramtum sent some linen garments to the palace in Mari (IX 129).

Of Zimri-Lim's other daughters little is known beyond the fact that they received rations from the palace stores.

Daughters of Other Kings

Little is preserved concerning the daughters of kings other than Zimri-Lim. Sumu-yamam, an obscure king who reigned after Yaḫdun-Lim on the throne of Mari,[51] is known to have had a daughter by the name of Takunḫatum (A.4634.9).[52] In a unique transaction, Ištar-tappi, the daughter of Yaḫdun-Lim,[53] borrowed ten shekels of silver from the temple of Šamaš; instead of interest she was to sacrifice two rams (to Šamaš; VII 48). In addition, Yaḫdun-Lim had many other daughters, for the Assyrian usurpers left behind correspondence concerning the disposition of some 18 daughters of Yaḫdun-Lim. In a letter to his son Yasmaḫ-Addu, Šamši-Adad counsels that the now grown daughters (SAL.TUR.MEŠ)[54] of Yaḫdun-Lim should be sent to Šubat-Enlil to learn the art of singing (*nārūtum*, I 64). In another letter (B 6), for which the address is lost but which is surely written to Yasmaḫ-Addu by one of his officials,[55] the writer recalls how the 18 daughters (TUR.SAL.MEŠ) of Yaḫdun-Lim had been given to him in compensation for some female slaves whom he had given to a third party. These 18 princesses are undoubtedly identical with the 18 women who in line 18 are called musicians (*zāmirātum*). Finet is certainly correct in equating these last women with those described in I 64.[56] It should be observed here that, while the royal origin of these princesses was remembered, their Assyrian masters did not treat them very differently from the other women who fell into their hands by right of conquest. They were given away to lesser officials in the same way as other slaves. In deference to their royal origin, however, they were not assigned to the textile industry, as were the majority of female captives.

Political Marriages

It is fitting to conclude this chapter on princesses with a word about political marriages. Dynastic marriages were common throughout the history of Mesopotamia as a means of forming or strengthening alliances. Perhaps in no period is its use so well documented as among the northern Mesopotamian kings during the Mari period.[57]

Among the best known of these dynastic marriages was the famous marriage Šamši-Adad arranged between his son Yasmaḫ-Addu and the daughter of the king of Qatna.[58] Šamši-Adad's son and successor, Išme-Dagan, in turn effectively utilized the political marriage to strengthen his power by taking the daughter of Zaziya, king of the Turukkū,[59] as wife for his son Mut-Aškur (II 40).

Zimri-Lim was himself the subject of such a marraige. He married Šibtu, the daughter of Yarim-Lim of Aleppo, king of Yamḫad. With the help of his father-in-law, Zimri-Lim wrested the throne of Mari from the control of the Assyrians. Despite some occasional misunderstandings, relations with the house of Yarim-Lim continued to be amicable for the duration of Zimri-Lim's reign, a situation no doubt due in part to the dynastic marriage involved.

Perhaps schooled by his own experience, Zimri-Lim regularly utilized the political marriage as part of his own imperial policy to secure his frontiers. It has already been observed how Zimri-Lim married off his daughter Tizpatum to Ili-Ištar, king of Šuna, and another daughter Kiru (and Šibatum ?) to Ḫaya-Sumu of Ilanṣura. Ibbatum was given to Ḫimdiya, the ruler of Andariq, and, if this writer's analysis is correct, Zimri-Lim arranged also for the marriage of his daughter Inib-šarri to Ibal-Addu of Ašlakka. All of these kinglets were located in the upper country in or neighboring Idamaraz. This whole area was in constant political ferment and subject to constantly shifting allegiance. The dynastic marriage was one part of Zimri-Lim's policy for bringing and keeping it under his hegemony.

In addition to those others treated above, Zimri-Lim may have given yet another daughter in a political marriage. In VI 26 Baḫdi-Lim reports the arrival in Mari of messengers from Aškur-Addu, king of Karana, opening negotiations for an alliance. Aškur-Addu, upon advice from his countrymen, offers to recognize Zimri-Lim as his suzerain, on the condition that the latter send his daughter in marriage.[60] The outcome of these negotiations is not preserved. But we may suppose that Zimri-Lim did not spurn this opportunity to expand his hegemony, since other documents reveal Aškur-Addu as an ally of Zimri-Lim.[61]

The difference between Zimri-Lim and his contemporaries in the use of the dynastic marriage to secure alliances, to judge from the available evidence, is that Zimri-Lim additionally invested his daughter-queens with real authority in their respective states. Sometimes, as in the case of Inib-šarri and Kiru, these marriages turned out to be unhappy ventures. But in a culture which institutionalized the subordination of women, the feelings of the woman involved were considered unimportant. Indeed, by contemporary standards, Zimri-Lim's policies regarding women, particularly the women of his own family, may be regarded as unusually enlightened.

NOTES TO CHAPTER 2

THE KINGS' DAUGHTERS

[1] For Inibšina, see below, chap. 4, pp. 59-61; for Erišti-Aja, see below, chap. 5.

[2] For a summary of relations between Zimri-Lim and Ibal-Addu of Ašlakka, see Finet, "Iawa-Ilâ, roi de Talḫayûm," *Syria* 41 (1964), 135-36. For the approximate location of Ašlakka, see Dossin, "A propos de la tablette administrative," *Syria* 41 (1964), 22; Finet, *Syria* 41 (1964), 135-36.

[3] Römer, *Frauenbriefe*, 49, restores *la ta-ba[-at*??*-ta*??*-]a-qi* "unter[brich (?? die Arbeit)] nicht," while Sasson, "Royal Ladies," 65, reads *ta-ba-[ak!]-ki* "do not cry."

[4] For the reading and interpretation of MU.DU, see Finet, *ARMT* XV, 218; Bottéro, VII, 208-10; Birot, IX, 253-54; see below, n. 16. Cf. further Edzard, *Altbabylonische Rechts- und Wirtschaftsurkunden aus Tell ed-Dēr im Iraq Museum, Baghdad* (München, 1970), 89.

[5] The passage is not without difficulties. Not only is the context cryptic, but also the scribe was unusually careless: *aš-šum ṭe*$_{4}$*-mi-im ša aš-pu-ra-ku-um / a-nu-um-ma ti-ir-ḫa-tum*(sic!) *a-na ṣe-er* / LUGAL *be-li*<*-ia*> *uš-ta-bi-lu-nim* "Concerning the report about which I wrote you--now they have brought the *terḫatum* to the king my lord." One wonders if the "5 (6?) mines of silver of the woman" referred to in line 22 is the amount of the *terḫatum*.

[6] Itur-Asdu began his career as a *barû* under Yasmaḫ-Addu. Under Zimri-Lim he was promoted to governor of Naḫur--the position he occupies in the present correspondence--and eventually to the governorship in Mari; see Dossin, "Revelation," *RA* 42 (1948), 125-26; Finet, *RA* 53 (1959), 68; *Rencontre XIV*, 92. Additional letters of Itur-Asdu have now been published by Dossin, *RA* 66 (1972), 115-20. See below, p. 67.

[7] The translation of II 113.4 by *CAD* Ṣ, 39, "gather (your household)" for *šutaṣbitī* is not appropriate, as implicitly recognized now in the revised translation of *CAD* K, 299. The parallel passage from X 76.5f.: *a-al-ki wa-ar[-ka-at] / [a]-wa-ti-ki pu-*⌈*ur*⌉*-s[i-ma]* "Go. Take care of your (own) affairs" seems to imply that Zimri-Lim was instructing his daughter to give her marriage and residence in Ašlakka another try before taking the drastic and final step of divorce and returning to her father at Mari.

[8] See de Vaux, "Sur le voile des femmes dans l'Orient ancien," *RB* 44 (1935), 397-412, reprinted in *Bible et Orient* (Paris, 1967), 407-23. See also Jastrow, *Revue Archéologique*, V^{e} série 14 (1921), 209-38; Driver and Miles, *The Assyrian Laws* (Oxford, 1935), 133-34.

[9] Contrary to de Vaux, "Sur le voile des femmes," 411, *qaqqada(m) katāmu* is not attested in the Middle Assyrian Laws. *qaqqada(m) katāmu/kuttumu* is, however, attested in later ritual and magical texts (see *CAD* K 299 and and 301; *CAD* Ṣ 224); but these passages do not bear on the question of veiling for a bride or wife.

[10] Nos. 40-41.

[11] Cf. *iktumma ibrī kīma kallati panū[šu]* "my friend veiled his face like a bride" (Gilgamesh VIII ii 17); cf. also *kallatum kuttumtum* "veiled bride" as an epithet of "Night" (*Maqlu* I 2; *KAR* 94,5; *JNES* 19 (1960), 32, l. 45; and 33, l. 53).

12 The one-sided view expressed by Inib-šarri is perhaps somewhat exaggeraged. In one text, Ibal-Addu requests news of Inib-šarri's well-being and perhaps is genuinely concerned: [š]*u-ul*-[*ma-am* š]*a i-ni-ib*-LUGAL / *šu-bi-li* "Send me news of Inib-šarri's well-being" (X 170.8-9). There are, however, no chronological indications in this text, so that it is impossible to be sure that it derives from the same period as Inib-šarri's letters.

13 We cannot prove that letters II 112-113 and X 76 written from Naḫur chronologically follow X 74, which tells of Inib-šarri's miseries in Ašlakka. Nevertheless a comparison of the letters seems to confirm our hypothesis: (1) *eli ša pānānu* "more than before" (II 113.23; cf. X 76.10) seems to refer to her miseries in Ašlakka; (2) the statement that she has not received sufficient food or firewood since leaving her father's presence (II 113.20-22) appears subsequent to the situation described in X 74.22f.; (3) Zimri-Lim's instructions to his daughter to go and take care of her house (in Ašlakka, II 113.4; X 76.5-6) refer apparently to a house which is already in her possession but from which she is now absent. Perhaps also relevant here is the passage in X 79.8-11: ⌈*i-na*⌉ *a-lim*^ki[i?]^ *ú-še-ṣú-ni-in*[*-ni*] *ù a-na na-ḫu-ur*^ki^ *at-ta-al-kam*! "They made me leave the city, and I went away to Naḫur"; the letter is broken, however, and no mention of Ibal-Addu is preserved.

14 See above, n. 7.

15 II 113.16-19; X 76.12-16.

16 Note the cautious statement of Birot, *ARMT* IX, 253, concerning the nature of MU.DU: "Les expéditeurs sont, en général, des personnages importants, comme dans les textes de la salle 110: princes vassaux ou alliés comme Šadû-Šarri et Šupram, hauts functionnaires (Ḫabdu-Malik, Meptûm, Zimri-Addu, Sammêtar), membres de la famille ou du harem royal (Narâmtum, Inib-šarri), collectivités locales (les "Anciens" de Zabalum, dans 241 8; cf. aussi les "Anciens" de Tizraḫ, dans VII, 130 2). Rien ne permet de discerner dans quelle mesure ces envois sont imposés ou librement consentis, ni d'apprécier leur périodicité. Notons que dans le n° 178, *MU.DU* ne désigne pas l'impôt lui-même, mais l'envoi de son montant qui en a été fait par les "precepteurs" (*bêl bilâtim*); de même dans I, 73 13, *MU.DU* désigne les sommes envoyées par le gouverneur de district au titre du tribut."

17 For additional information on Inib-šarri, see Sasson, "Royal Ladies," 63-67.

18 On the location of Ilanṣura, see O. Rouault, "Andariq et Atamrum," *RA* 64 (1970), 108-9.

19 On Ḫaya-Sumu, see Huffmon, *APNM*, 32f.; Römer, *Frauenbriefe*, 7, with n. 4; add XII 747.15.

20 On the tenuousness of Zimri-Lim's control of this area, see XIII 143 and the commentary by Finet, *Syria* 41 (1964), 136-37; *RA* 60 (1966), 23.

21 *ḫazannūtam wašābum* is elsewhere approximated by the NA *šākin māti*...LÚ *rēšišu ana* LÚ *ḫazannūti ussēšib* "(after the death of the king) the governor of the country installed his officer as mayor" *ABL* 473:6 (tr. *CAD* Ḫ 166); however, *ḫazannum wašābum* is common at Mari: *wašāb ḫazannim ūl rittum* "the seating of a mayor is not opportune" II 137.47; LU *ḫazanni ina* URU.KI [*šêt*]*u wašib* "he sits as the mayor in that city" II 109.9.

22 *anninum* is a variant of *annānum* "here"; see Laessøe, *Shemshara Tablets*,

SH 856:7, with commentary, and *CAD* A^2 131f.

23 As does Moran, in a private communication.

24 Sasson, "Royal Ladies," 69, acknowledges that the author is either Kiru or Šibatum, and tentatively credits it to the latter. It is unlikely that Šibatum is the author, however, because the letter's contents are inconsistent with Šibatum's dossier but quite in line with Kiru's professed activities.

25 Zu-ḫatni, in the opinion of Rouault, *RA* 64 (1970), 108, was the commander of the army of Ḫaya-Sumu. See II 79.6-8, where he heads the combined forces of Ḫaya-Sumu and Šubram, the king of Kirdaḫat. However, in IX 298.12, he seems to be another of the several kinglets in the country of Idamaraz, despite the objection of Birot, *ARMT* IX, 348.

26 In VII 226.39 Yarim-Dagan is identified as LÚ *du-un-ni-im*[ki]; cf. XII 239.5. In XIII 107 we learn that this man has changed residence from Dunnum to Ilum-muluk and that Zimri-Lim has given orders for his secret liquidation. No reason is given for his fall into disfavor.

27 This letter has been treated by Dossin, "Documents de Mari," *Syria* 48 (1971), 7-8; "Une capture de lion au Habour d'après une lettre de Mari," *BARB* 56 (1970), 313.

28 [*i*]*-na-an-na ù šum-ma a-na-ku sí-ni-ša-ku* / [*a-b*]*i ù be-lì a-na a-wa-ti-ia* / [*l*]*i-qú-ul* (ll. 7´-9´). For the concessive meaning of *u šumma*, see Moran, *Biblica* 50 (1969), 31, note on X 8.9. See further X 90.29; 101.16.

29 Perhaps relevant to Kiru's role as an administrator is the passage in which she tells her father: *ša-ni-tam a-nu-um-ma* 32 LÚ.TUR.MEŠ *ša i-na* É *ma-ri*[ki] *wa-aš-bu* ⌜*iš*⌝*-tu i-na-an-na a-na e-pê-eš* É*-tim ša-a-ti qa-ti aš-ku-un* "Another matter. Now the 32 valets who are residing in Mari--from this moment I myself have undertaken to organize that house" (X 31.14´-17´). However, it is unclear to me whether this activity is being undertaken in Mari (after Kiru's return there) or in Ilanṣura. Cf. Römer, *Frauenbriefe*, 68; Sasson, "Royal Ladies," 68. See also n. 39, below.

30 Or Šimatum. The reading of this name is uncertain, see Artzi-Malamat, *Or* 40 (1971), 77, n. 7.

31 "Royal Ladies," 68-72; *BiOr* 28 (1971), 355.

32 Parallel to *ana mārtūtim*, perhaps one should read *ana mārūtim* instead of *ana aplūtim*; on the ambivalence of DUMU.UŠ as *aplu* or *māru*, see *CAD* A^2 176 b.

33 This cannot be translated "It is you who has made me as daughter and as heiress," as does Sasson, "Royal Ladies," 69. While our passage is not identical, it approximates the expression *ana mārtūtim nadānum*, "to give (up) for adoption." I know of no corroborating evidence to justify Sasson's translation.

34 Cf. XIII 101.6-22, where in a context of marriage negotiations, a similar expression occurs (l. 18).

35 For the reading of l. 14, see von Soden, *Or* 22 (1953), 201.

36 This letter was treated by Moran, *Biblica* 50 (1969) 43f.; cf. Sasson, "Royal Ladies," 71f.

37 Sasson, "Royal Ladies," 70f.

[38] The expression *ištu pāni* X *amārum* is otherwise not attested. Translation is from context.

[39] Additional documentation concerning Kiru may still be forthcoming, since Finet (*Rencontre XVIII*, 69) claims that Kiru "paraît avoir géré les affaires du palais après la mort de sa mère Šibtu, et, sans doute, avant la relève matrimoniale qu'assurera Addu-dûri." Nevertheless, the only evidence cited is X 31, 14′-17′, which seems insufficient to support such a large claim, involving as it does the further hypothesis of Šibtu's death and subsequent replacement by Addu-dûri. See above, n. 29.

[40] This daughter of Zimri-Lim is not the author of X 105; in that letter, a Tizpatum calls herself "your daughter" to Dariš-libur, but this appears to be nothing more than an expression of deference before a high echelon official. The seal of this same (?) Tizpatum is mentioned in X 116.30. So also Sasson, "Royal Ladies," 72, n. 66.

[41] See already Römer, *Frauenbriefe*, 39f.

[42] The copy has *a*-NAM, which Römer, in *ibid.*, has interpreted as "gewiss (?)." In a private communication, Moran comments, "The mysterious *a-nam* of 11.5 and 10 cannot, I believe, be more than a mistake for *a-lam*!"; similarly Dossin, *RA* 64 (1970), 163. M. Stol *apud* Sasson, *BiOr* 28 (1971), 356, reads *a-lam*$_x$ and also in l. 7 *tàk-lam*$_x$.

[43] Or "strong (*dan-nam*)"; see preceding note.

[44] For a similar expression of subservience, cf. *ma-a-tam an-ni-tum* [*š*]*a a-na ṣe-ri-šu-nu ú-zu-un-ša tu-ur-ra-at id-da-ni-in it-ti-šu-nu it-ta-ki-ir* "this country which was subservient to them reinforced itself and opened hostilities with them" (IV 24.20-23).

[45] Dossin, "L'ordalie à Mari," *CRAIB* (1958), 388. See also Dossin, "Ḫattuša dans une lettre de Mari," *RHA* tome 5, fasc. 35 (1939), 72, where Ili-Ištar protests his loyalty to his "father" Zimri-Lim; and IX 298.8. Perhaps this same person is referred to under the variant PN *i-la*-IŠDAR (VII 199.22′). See now Sasson, "Royal Ladies," 72-74.

[46] II 62. See above, p. 42, with n. 20. On the location of Šuna, see Finet, *ARMT* XV, 135.

[47] See below, chap. 4, pp. 86-87.

[48] An unnamed daughter (SAL.TUR) of the king, surely Zimri-Lim, is mentioned in another ration list (VII 206.10′). Presumably she is one of the princesses already known from elsewhere.

X 47, a badly broken tablet, contains the message of one ^{f}ia-x[ ] DUMU.MÍ-*tá-ka*[*-a(-ma)*], reporting that she was robbed. That this letter was addressed to Zimri-Lim is not certain.

[49] Sasson, "Royal Ladies," 62-63.

[50] Text treated by Römer, *Frauenbriefe*, 53-55.

[51] Sumu-yamam can now be shown to have reigned after Yaḫdun-Lim, thus eliminating the uncertainty of Dossin, *RA* 64 (1970), 18. A recently published text (Dossin, "Deux lists nominatives du règne de Sûmu-Iamam," *RA* 65 [1971], 55) lists a PN *ša Dûr-Ia-aḫ-du-li-im* (A.3562. xiii.27). This text is dated [*Šanat Su-m*]*u-ia-ma-am* [*Ḫa-la-bi-it*(?)]^{ki} [*i-pu*]*-šu* "Year in which Sumu-yamam built Ḫalabit(?)." Obviously, then, the reign of the king after whom the fortress was named was chronologically prior to that of Sumu-yamam.

[52]See *RA* 64 (1970), 43.

[53]Boyer (*ARMT* VIII, 70, n. 2), on the contrary, argues that this woman cannot be the daughter of the king of Mari by that name, since it is difficult to imagine her falling into such straits that she would need to borrow from the temple. It seems to this writer, however, that the unusual character of the loan, especially the matter of interest, requires the opposite conclusion.

[54]See below, n. 56.

[55]Finet, "Une lettre de récriminations au vice-roi de Mari, Iasmaḫ-Addu," *AIPHOS* 15 (1958-60), 17-32, esp. 25f.

[56]*Ibid.*, 26-27. Absolute certainty cannot be had, however, as to whether these women were the real daughters of Yaḫdun-Lim. Caution is required because of the variation in the writing of the logogram, SAL.TUR (I 64) and TUR.SAL (B6). SAL.TUR normally stands for *ṣuḫārtum* or the like; however, on occasion it stands for *mārtum* in place of normal TUR.SAL, as in I 46.11; VII 206.10 ; X 26.6. The weight of the argument in favor of reading *mārātum* because of the writing TUR.SAL in B6 may be negated by the multiple occurrences of TUR.SAL in that same text in situations where *ṣuḫārātum* may well be intended.

[57]Korošec, "Les relations internationales d'après les lettres de Mari," *Rencontre XV*, 142; Bottéro, *La femme*, 212; J. M. Munn-Rankin, "Diplomacy in Western Asia," *Iraq* 18 (1956), 94-95.

[58]I 24; 46; 77; A.2548 (=*BARB* 40 [1954], 422); cf. II 51.

[59]On Zaziya, see Laessøe, *The Shemshara Tablets*, 40-42; Page, "The Tablets from Tell-al-Rimah 1967," *Iraq* 30 (1968), 89-90.

[60]Perhaps one should compare here the reference to the setting up of the king's throne in Andariq, X 165.13-15.

[61]This conclusion is strengthened by the presence at Mari of the Karana princess(?) Belassunu and related incidents; see below, chap. 3, pp. 61-64. On the possibility of still other political marriages arranged by Zimri-Lim, see Sasson, "Royal Ladies," 74.

CHAPTER 3

OTHER SERVANTS OF THE KING

This chapter is devoted to women who exercise important roles at Mari but who do not belong to the immediate royal family or the harem. The titles and/or background of some of these women are known (Inibšina and Belassunu); but for others no exact titles or even functions can be determined (Addu-duri and Ama-dugga).

Inibšina, a Governor's Wife

Tracing the prosopography of Inibšina is not easy since there was more than one well-placed Inibšina at Mari and one does not always know which material to correlate with which person. That there were at least two women bearing the name Inibšina is obvious, as they are mentioned together on the same tablet: Inibšina the *ugbabtum* of Adad (C i.4-5)[1] and another Inibšina who is given no specific title or other qualification (C i.20). Further, it is known that the wife of Baḫdi-Lim, the sometime governor of Mari under Zimri-Lim, was named Inibšina.[2] As a married women this last-named lady cannot be identified with Inibšina the *ugbabtum*;[3] whether she is identical with Inibšina of C i.20 is at the present time difficult to determine. However, this writer sees no reason to assume more than one person here and so, on the principal of economy, tentatively identifies them as one and the same person. Sasson also identifies them, but contrary to his opinion,[4] there is insufficient evidence for postulating that this Inibšina is a princess, the daughter of Zimri-Lim. In fact the available evidence is against such an assumption, since Inibšina's name in the ration list (C i.20) is explicitly placed *after* the names of those women identified as princesses (DUMU.MÍ.MEŠ LUGAL, C i.4-17). As the wife of the governor she was one of the noble ladies of Mari, which is sufficient reason for placing her immediately after the princesses and the wife or wives of the king. She may even have been related to the king, as the familiar tone of her correspondence with him suggests.[5]

Among the feminine correspondence are four letters (X 80-83) written by an Inibšina. Although certainty is not possible, it seems that these letters are to be credited to Inibšina, the governor's wife, rather than to Inibšina the *ugbabtum*. This assumption is made primarily on the basis of the writer's professed activities, which involve both administrative duties and the supervision of religious personnel. Such activities are more suited to a governor's wife than a priestess. It is my opinion that Zimri-Lim utilized this wife of the governor in an administrative role analogous to the way in which he employed his queen and secondary wife or wives.

In X 82 (cf. XIII 14) Inibšina is connected with the archives building (*bīt tuppātim*). The king sent orders that Inibšina was to open the archives for Mukannišum and Ṭabat-šarrussu by breaking the seal on the door. Later she reseals it and sends the seal to the king. Like Šibtu on a similar occasion,[6] Inibšina here functions as the king's personal representative in an important administrative matter. One might argue, however, that Inibšina was less confident of her own personal authority than Šibtu, who felt no compulsion to send the seal on to the king so as to guarantee the integrity of the sealing and preclude any suspicion of tampering. At the end of the letter (lines 21-23) Inibšina mentions that she is sending the king a chair and a footstool inlaid with alabaster. These items were apparently personal gifts from Inibšina rather than supplies sent in the capacity of an administrator. Such munificence was certainly not detrimental to her influence with the king.

X 83 is too broken to yield any coherent picture. In her two remaining letters, Inibšina is seen forwarding oracles to the king. In X 80 she recalls that previously she had reported an oracle (*têrtum*) which Šelibum, the cult player (*assinnum*), had given her for the king. Now she reports to the king an oracle given her by the "speaker (*qabbātum*) of Dagan of Terqa"[7] concerning the deceptiveness of the peace initiatives of the king of Ešnunna. In X 81 Inibšina forwards to the king an oracle delivered by Innibana, the prophetess (*āpiltum*). In all three cases these lesser religious personnel delivered their messages for the king to Inibšina: "Šelibum, the cult player, gave me (*iddinam*) an oracle and I wrote you"; "The speaker of Dagan of Terqa came and said to me (*illikamma ki'am iqbêm*)"; the third may have been delivered publicly but was also communicated directly to Inibšina, "I hereby give you (*addinakkim*) my lock (of hair) and my fringe." Inibšina in each case is seen as a proper authority to whom one delivers an oracle intended for the king. Her role again seems to be much the same as that of the queen in similar circumstances.[8]

Inibšina's activities may have extended into other areas as well, for presumably this is the same Inibšina who in unpublished legal texts from Mari is engaged in vast commercial activities involving grain.[9] Final judgment must, however, be suspended until more information is available.

From the above analysis it may be concluded that, like the queen, Inibšina actively engaged in the extraordinary administration of the palace. Her role, however, was much more circumscribed than that of the queen. Nevertheless there is sufficient evidence for postulating that Zimri-Lim often, if not regularly, employed Inibšina for such extraordinary duties. This is, of course, of a piece with an emerging pattern of the reign of Zimri-Lim. It would help in our assessment of this king's attitude toward women if Inibšina's exact relationship to the king were known. Is she nothing more than a governor's wife who has personally ingratiated herself with the king, or did the status of being the governor's wife itself carry some institutionalized influence with the king? Not to be excluded, however, is the possibility that Inibšina was recommended to the king because she was a relative, although, to be sure, consanguinity was not an essential ingredient for ascendancy in Mari.

Belassunu

At one time it was believed that this woman was one of the secondary wives of Zimri-Lim.[10] However, as Sasson has convincingly demonstrated, this Belassunu must be identified with the woman of that name known from the Tell al-Rimah letters and hence cannot be a wife of the Mari monarch.[11] Nevertheless, Sasson's reconstruction of the prosopography of this woman is ill conceived, as will be evident shortly.

Most of our biographical information about Belassunu derives from a letter from Tell al-Rimah--a site believed to be ancient Karana. According to TR 4251, Belassunu is the wife of one Abdu-šuri--although unhappily married--and the mother of children:

> To Iltani speak: thus (says) ᶠAz-zu-[X]. Don't keep writing to me about Belassunu. That woman does not want to live here with her husband, so let her go with her children to her brother-in-law's house. You there are near, while I am far away and cannot write to Mutu-ḫadki. That woman wants to go to Andariq. Furthermore, Abdu-šuri her husband constantly ill-treats her, and as long as that woman is near me, I am pestered with her complaints.[12]

Belassunu is mentioned also in a letter to Iltani from her husband Ḫaqbu-Ḫammu:

> Speak to Iltani: thus Aqba-ḫammu. Let them open (*or*, unseal) the ice of Qaṭara. The goddess, you and Belassunu drink regularly, and make sure that the ice is guarded (TR 4097).[13]

That this Belassunu is the same person as the one known from Mari is proved by X 174, written by Ḫaqba-Ḫammu to Belassunu, which alludes to her house and children back in Karana. Before considering this letter in detail, however, it will be advantageous to recall that at Mari Belassunu is also attested elsewhere as receiving rations. In *Tablette C* she, along with other noble ladies, is rationed a generous amount of oil, while in VII 206.9′ she is allotted a choice cut of meat, always a rare commodity in those days.

But what is one to make of this data? Sasson would have Belassunu be a daughter of Zimri-Lim who was given in marriage by her father in another of his political alliances to a prince of Karana, the aforementioned Abdu-šuri. After an unhappy marriage, the supposed Mari princess eventually returns to her native city. But before that, Ḫaqba-Ḫamma usurps the throne of the rightful heir (?), Abdu-šuri, his own brother-in-law, all the while maintaining amicable relations with Zimri-Lim and his daughter Belassunu. Sasson's reconstruction is less than convincing.

There is not one shred of evidence that Belassunu is Zimri-Lim's daughter. The fact that she received one *qa* of oil as her ration in *Tablette C* is hardly evidence that she is a princess, as Sasson argues, for the princesses receive varying amounts, 1 1/2 *qa*, 1 *qa*, and 2/3 *qa* (lines 4-17). More damaging to Sasson's argument, however, Belassunu is not listed among those women explicitly named as princesses (lines 4-17) but is listed *after* them (line 21). This removes any compelling reason to suppose that Belassunu might have been the princess sent in reply to Aškur-Addu's request to ally by marriage the royal houses of Mari and Karana (VI 26). Moreover, from TR 4251 it appears that Belassunu's brother-in-law was not Ḫaqba-Ḫammu but Mutu-ḫadki in Andariq, thus making unlikely a supposition that Belassunu's husband was a prince of Karana. Lastly, nothing requires us to suppose that Ḫaqba-Ḫammu was ever the ruler or king of Karana, as Sasson supposes. It is sufficient to postulate that Ḫaqba-Ḫammu, as husband of the native princess Iltani, was a high official in Karana, perhaps even governor in that city. Such a position more than accounts for the nature of his correspondence.

In my opinion, S. Page is probably correct in assuming that Belassunu is the sister of Iltani and therefore also a Karana princess.[14] This makes obvious why in TR 4251 Iltani's correspondent ^{f}Az-zu-X, who both lives far from Karana and surely has some authoritative relationship to Belassunu, is unknown among the royal women of Mari. It seems, too, that Belassunu succeeded in her desire to go to Andariq.[15] Eventually, by some unknown route, she made her way to Mari, which was now allied with her homeland. While in Mari she was well attended, in keeping with her status as visiting royalty, witness the generous portions allotted her.

It is this context that is reflected in the sole surviving letter of Belassunu's Mari correspondence (X 174).

a-na ^{f}*be-la-sú-nu*
qí-bí-ma
[*u*]*m-ma aq-bu-am-mu-ú ma-ru*$^{?!}$*-ki-ma*
[*š*]*a-al-ma-ku ia*$_8$-⸢*tar*⸣*-sa-lim* ⸢*ša*⸣*-lim*
DUMU.MEŠ-*ki ka-lu-*⸢*šu-nu*⸣
ša-al-mu É-*ki* ⸢*ša*⸣*-lim*
a-nu-[*u*]*m-ma*
aš-šum ṭe$_4$*-em*
at-lu-ki-[*ia*]
tup-pa-am a-na [*ṣe-er*]
be-lí-ia uš-ta-bi-il

ù a-na ṣe-er a-bi-ia
^{m}*ḫa-mu-ša-ki-iš uš-ta-bi-il*
at-ti aš-ra-nu-um
⌜*du*⌝*-ub-bi-bi-ma*
1[+1(?)] LÚ.MEŠ *a-mi-ru*
ka(?)*-lu-tum*
it-ti ia-mu-ud-ḫa-ma-ad
ar-ḫi-iš
⌜*li*⌝*-iḫ-mu-ṭú-nim*

To Belassunu say, thus (says) Ḫaqba-Ḫammu your son(?):[16] I am well. Yatar-salim is well. All your sons are well. Your house is well. Now then concerning [my] leaving, I have sent a letter to my lord and I have sent (a letter) to my father (through) Ḫamu-šagiš. You yourself there put in a word so that two(?) lightly armed scouts(?) come in utmost haste with Yamud-ḫamad.

Ḫaqba-Ḫammu is obviously writing to his superior. After reporting on the condition of her family and household back home, Ḫaqba-Ḫammu gets around to the real purpose of the letter, his imminent journey. It is manifest that he is to undertake the journey at the request of Belassunu; apparently he is to come to Mari and escort his lady back to her own city and household. To this end he has written requesting permission both of his own "lord," i.e., the king of Karana Aškur-Addu, and of his "father," i.e., Zimri-Lim, to whom Karana was in vassalage. Zimri-Lim was probably away on a campaign at the time, because the message was delivered to him through the official Ḫamu-šagiš, a person who elsewhere is represented as leading armies in the vicinity of Qattunan and eastward across the Tigris[17] and so was in contact with Zimri-Lim. We have no information on the further activities of Belassunu, but presumably she eventually returned to her own city and household.

Addu-duri

Another woman who enjoyed great prestige with Zimri-Lim was Addu-duri. She was often pressed into service for one of his special projects. In addition, her actions and correspondence indicate that she must have served in some kind of official capacity in Mari. As Addu-duri's identity is perplexing, we shall analyze her function before taking up the question of her status and relationship to the royal family.

Although we are unable to determine her exact title, Addu-duri seemingly served in an official capacity with jurisdiction over a broad area. Her jurisdiction included the palace and the temples, as is readily evident from her correspondence. These were the areas with which she was most closely involved. Nevertheless, her jurisdiction was not limited to the palace and the temples but included the whole of the capital city. In her official reports to the king, Addu-duri reports primarily on the well-being of the palace (X 54.4-5; 55.5; cf. 57.6) but may include her other areas of responsibility as well: *a-l[um m]a-ri*^ki^ É.ḪI.A DINGIR.MEŠ.ḪI.A [*ša-al-ma* É].GAL*-lum ša-lim* "The city Mari and the temples of the gods are safe, the palace is safe" (X 54.4-5). These are the same kinds of reports that other officials in Mari, and in particular the queen, send to the king.[18]

The palace and its direction come up specifically in letter X 57. Addu-duri is hard put to answer the palace servants (*gerseqqu*) who have come to her for an explanation. One of their fellow servants who has served in the palace from the time he was a youth is about to be given away callously to someone else as a gift now that he is an old man. But our interest is not in the heartless uprooting of a loyal servant past his prime. It is in the fact that the man's fellows come to Addu-duri to complain. They recognize her as the king's official from whom an accounting is due. However the decision was not hers, and she had to submit the grievance to the king for redress. This letter confirms that Addu-duri's place of residence was in the palace (line 6). So what is elsehwere called the "house of Addu-duri" (XI 68.6-7; XII 141.15; 146.4-5) is in all likelihood a part of the palace.[19]

Addu-duri's other major area of jurisdiction, the temples and related cultic matters, occasions many letters. Like other important officials, she transmits with relative frequency various prophetic messages to the king. In X 50 she transmits the ominous oracle of the *muḫḫutum* in the temple of Annunitum, along with the legally required symbols of the prophetess.[20] She proceeds similarly in the case of the *āpilum* who prophesied in the temple of Ḫišametum (X 53). Additionally, the woman Timlu reports portents to Addu-duri, "her mistress" (X 117). The *šangûm* of the temple of Itur-Mer also reports to her, as can be inferred from X 51, in which she sends his dream to Zimri-Lim. Nor does she omit her own ominous dream (X 50.3-21).

Addu-duri's responsibility in matters of the official cult is particularly evident in the incident involving the construction of a throne in the temple of Annunitum. The king had, so it seems, determined to adorn the temple door with some golden *tulū*,[21] a proposal which meets with the disapproval of the temple administrator.[22] The deliberation is recorded in X 52:

⌜*a*⌝-*na be-lí-ia*
qí-bí-ma
um-ma ^{fd}IM-*du-ri*
GEMÉ-*ka-a-ma*
aš-š[*u*]*m tu-le-e* [G]UŠKIN
[*š*]*a*? *an-nu-ni-tim*
^{m}*a-ḫu-um* LÚ.SANGA
il-li-ka-am-ma
ki-a-am iq-bi-e-em
um-ma-mi a-na na-[*da*]*-ni-im*
ú-ul ri-it-t[*u-u*]*m*
iš-tu-ma GIŠ.GU.ZA *ša il-tim*
in-ne-ep-pí-šu
te-er-tum li-in-ne-pí-iš-ma
GUŠKIN-*šu li-il-l*[*i*]*-qé-ma*
a-na GIŠ.GU.ZA *ša il-tim*
li-in-ne-pí-iš

To my lord say, thus (says) Addu-duri, your servant: Concerning the golden *tulū* of[23] Annunitum, Aḫum the temple administrator came to me and said as follows: "It is not appropriate to give (it)." If indeed the throne of the goddess is to be constructed, let an omen be taken and then let its gold be taken and made into the throne of the goddess.

Aḫum's objection was sustained. The question was submitted to the deity for an answer. The outcome is given in another of Addu-duri's letters to the king:

ša-ni-tam i-nu-ma
SISKUR$_x$.RE GIŠ.GU.[Z]A
ša É *an-nu-ni-tim*
SISKUR$_x$.RE *aq-qí-ma*
t[e-r]e-tum ma-di-iš!
d[am?-q]a? i-na 1 *te-er-tim*
a-[ša]-al-lu
⌜i⌝[-na] ša-ni-tim
a-ša!-al lu[-ma? e?-p]u?-úš

Another matter. At the time of the sacrifice for the throne of the temple of Annunitum, I offered sacrifice. And the omens were very favorable(?). I consulted with one omen; I consulted with a second.[24] Then I proceeded(?). (X 55.12-20)

If our reading of the text is correct, Addu-duri ends by stating that she proceeded to carry out the will of the deity as expressed in the omens. Be that as it may, it is perfectly obvious that Addu-duri has proceeded throughout the incident as the king's responsible officer in charge of such matters. Aḫum came to her first to complain; Addu-duri consults the king for instructions. She then initiates the sacrifices and accompanying omen-taking to arrive at a decision.

Thanks to a most fortuitous reconstruction of events related to the visit of Simaḫlane, king of Kurda, in Mari, Birot has succeeded in delineating the concerns of several officials.[25] At the time the king was away in Dur-Yaḫdun-Lim but was expected to depart for Mari in time for the sacrifice to the goddess Diritum (X 142.22-27). The letters of the several parties reveal that Itur-Asdu, now the governor in Mari, and Yasim-Sumu the *šadubba* were concerned primarily with preparations for the royal guest, questions of food, lodging, security, protocol, and the like. In the meanwhile Zimri-Lim sent instructions to Addu-duri to make ready the coming sacrifice to Diritum, strictly charging her:

tup-pí an-né-e-em i-na še-me-em
ṭe$_4$*-em* SISKUR$_x$.RE.ḪI.A
ša ^{d}*di-ri-tim lu! šu-ta-aṣ-bu-ut*
a-ḫu-um la in-na-ad-di

Upon (your) hearing this tablet of mine, let plans be made

for the sacrifice of Diritum. Do not be negligent!
(X 142.28-31).

Birot has drawn attention to the fact that throughout these preparations there was little communication between the three officials in Mari. Each operated in isolation from the other, corresponding directly with the absent king about his own jurisdictional affairs only. Additional documents confirm that Zimri-Lim did arrive on schedule. He and his royal guest Simaḫlane went the short distance to Dir to offer the sacrifice to the goddess and to partake of the festivities. After three days they returned to Mari. We are left in the dark as to Addu-duri's role during the actual offering of the sacrifice.

Addu-duri's concern with omens and sacrifices is taken up again in other texts. In X 54 she cautions the king not to be negligent in guarding himself but to proceed in accordance with the favorable omens--omens which she evidently has sent him (cf. X 142.4f.). In X 144 the king acknowledges a letter from Addu-duri in which she had affirmed her diligence in seeing to the sacrifices in the temples of all the gods (SISKUR$_{x}$.RE. ḪI.A É DINGIR.MEŠ); and Zimri-Lim then cautions her against any future laxity in this matter. It is apparent from these passages that Addu-duri is acting on the king's behalf and has the responsibility for seeing that the official cult is properly conducted while the king is away from Mari.

Knowledge of Addu-duri's official capacity illuminates other more cryptic passages. In one letter to Addu-duri, Zimri-Lim announces that he will set out from Ziniyan to appear before Dagan of Ṣubatum, where he will satisfy the demands of the god:

pa-ni [d]*da-gan ša ṣú-ba-tim*[ki]
at-ta-na-ap-la-ás
ù ḫi-ṭi-ti-šu
ma-li i-ri-ša-an-ni
a-na-ad-di-in
u-ul a-ka-la

I will look continually upon the face of Dagan of Ṣubatim and I will give (him) his compensation,[26] however much he has requested of me. I will not withhold (anything). (X 143.13-18)

If our interpretation is correct, the sanctuary of Dagan at Ṣubatum has suffered some injury. It is impossible to say whether the king was in any way negligent or responsible. In any case the king promises to make good any damage when he visits the sanctuary. However, it is Addu-duri's role in the matter which interests us. That the king should assure her that the affair will be taken care of may mean she had a special interest in this sanctuary. At the minimum it confirms Addu-duri's close connection with the official cult.[27]

Another text (XI 68) seems to say that Addu-duri furnished certain cereals for cultic use for the *qilusatum* feast.[28] This is a receipt for items furnished from the "house" of Addu-duri for the *qilusatum*; it apparently refers to items furnished in her capacity as an official, not as a private person.

If the preceding texts establish Addu-duri's close supervision of and responsibility for the official cult, other texts confirm that her official duties also included secular affairs. That she exercised some kind of jurisdiction over the palace has already been established. It is as an administrator of the palace that Addu-duri controled various kinds of supplies. On one occasion when wool was in short supply in Mari, Mukannišum wrote to the king asking that a sack of special Babylonian wool sealed with the king's own seal be opened. So he requests, "Let my lord write to Addu-duri that this sack be opened in front of her..." (XIII 10.15-17). As an overseer of the textile industry Mukannišum had a legitimate interest in these wool supplies.[29] Addu-duri's role is less clear; seemingly her presence was to preclude any action detrimental to the interests of the crown.

Addu-duri was also active in various legal matters. In another group of texts Addu-duri investigated disputes over property and money for the king. In II 114 she reviewed (*sanāqum*) the claims of two parties to an estate(?) belonging to a brother of one of the parties and then sent the case to the king for settlement. In X 58 she was again reviewing (*sunnuqum*) a case concerning a sum of money. One party claimed that a deposit of money had been left in the keeping of the other but could produce no evidence to substantiate the claim. Although not explicitly stated, Addu-duri also sent this case to the king for his judgment.[30]

Addu-duri was, in addition, a capable administrator. Zimri-Lim called upon her to accomplish certain tasks for him. Two letters from Zimri-Lim contain his instructions to Addu-duri commissioning her to have ceremonial weapons(?) made for him. The earlier letter gives us the details:

a-na ^{fd}IM-*du-ri*
qí-bí-ma
um-ma be-el-ki-i-ma
i-na ki-ir-re-et KÙ.BABBAR *ra-ab-bi-e-tim*
ša ḫa-a-ià-⸢i⸣-lu-ú
ú-ša-bi-la-ak-ki-im
1 *ki-ir-re* KÙ.BABBAR *ra-bi-im-ma*
li-qí-e-ma
⸢*x*⸣ [*š*]*a-ti wa-ki-il* LÚ.[ ]
[ ].MEŠ *be-e-e*[*l*]
ù ki-ir-re[*-tim ša-ni-tim*]
šu-ta-aṣ-b[*i-ti-ma*]
a-na DUMU.MEŠ U[RUDU$^{?}$.NAGAR$^{?}$]
id-ni-[*ma*]
8 *ka!-ak-ki-i* KÙ.BABB[AR]
ša 2/3 ÀM MA.NA
li-pu-šu-ma
ar-ḫi-iš a-na ṣe-ri-ia
li-ša-ak-ši-du-nim
[*a-na na*]*-aš-pa-ar-ti-ia an-ni-tim*
⸢*a*⸣*-ḫi-ki la ta-na-ad-di-i*

To Addu-duri say, thus (says) your lord: From the large silver jugs, which Ḫaya-ilu sent to you, take 1 large silver jug and.....But prepare(?), so that they can make 8 silver weapons (weighing) 2/3 mine each. And then have them quickly brought to me. Do not be negligent (in carrying out) this order of mine! (X 146)

A subsequent letter (X 145) recalls Addu-duri's reply to this order (lines 4-11), which may have been an objection that there was insufficient metal to make the prescribed weapons. Zimri-Lim's answer is lost. These letters confirm Addu-duri's capacity as an official of the king. In the first place, the fact that Ḫaya-ilu sent the vessels intended for the king to Addu-duri demonstrates that this provincial king(?) knew that

Addu-duri was the proper official to receive such gifts. The fact that these vessels were already under the direction of Addu-duri may explain why the king sent the instructions for converting them into ceremonial weapons to her. But it also proves that she had an office and the authority to accomplish such matters. Therefore it is also likely that other broken letters, were they better preserved, would reveal her administrative powers in other areas; she had some hand in the matter of white horses from Qatanum (X 147) and was concerned about runaway palace slaves (X 60) and slaves who had escaped from the prison (X 150).

Addu-duri's office entailed obligations as well as power. Several receipts are preserved which record grain delivered to Ilukanum, the overseer of the palace stores, "from the house of Addu-duri" (XII 141.15; 146; 242). These contributions were evidently a kind of tax expected in view of the wealth derived from her royal appointment. XII 141 includes her with other royal appointees--vassal kings or high officials--who contributed to the palace stores. Furthermore, if text IX 237 were preserved complete, Addu-duri's name would surely appear on that tablet as well, since many of the names of the officials of the realm are the same as on XII 141.

The importance of Addu-duri cannot be doubted. She ranks among the high officials of Mari. Zimri-Lim trusted in her abilities. Indeed, she would at times appear to rival the queen in the amount of confidence the king placed on her, for she performed many of the same functions as the queen in both cultic and secular affairs. Addu-duri, however, did not enjoy the personal prerogatives of the queen; she had no power which she exercised independently of an explicit royal command. Nor did Addu-duri's authority extend beyond the city of Mari, as did the queen's. In short, her authority was not nearly as pervasive as the queen's. Just the same, she remains an unusually powerful woman in the reign of Zimri-Lim.

But who was this Addu-duri? As already stated, her official title is unknown. Impressions of her seal reportedly read *(il)Addu-du-r*[*i*]/ *amat Ḫa-ad-ni-Èl* "Addu-duri, servant of Ḫadni-El."[31] Should this be the correct reading, Addu-duri would be the servant of an obscure figure--perhaps an army commander--named Ḫatni-El/Ḫatni-iluma.[32] However, it is almost certain that the name of Addu-duri's master is incomplete. The correct reading of the seal would appear to be ⌜f⌝^{d}IM-*du-r*[*i*] / [G]EMÉ *ḫa-at-ni*-^{d}[x].[33] Of the possible candidates, the name of Ḫatni-^{d}Addu appears most likely. According to an unpublished text, Ḫatni-Addu was a king of some unspecified region who lost his life in battle.[34] If Addu-duri was a servant of this king, she must have made her way to Mari--or was taken there--after the death of her master. Zimri-Lim may have recognized her talents and employed her in his service.

On the other hand, there is the possibility that Addu-duri came with Zimri-Lim and Šibtu from Aleppo at the time Zimri-Lim regained the throne of his father. From the correspondence of Šibtu with her father, Yarim-Lim king of Aleppo, it emerges that Šibtu was particularly interested in the fortunes of one Ḫatni-Addu. She requested of her father that a certain field be given to this man to cultivate. Yarim-Lim responded that, due to unfortunate circumstances, this was not possible; however, he would give him a comparable field (X 151).[35] The queen's interest in this particular man could provide the link to Addu-duri's importance under Zimri-Lim. If Addu-duri was his servant and Ḫatni-Addu was a favorite of Queen Šibtu and Zimri-Lim, then Addu-duri perhaps received peferential treatment because of her master's favor at the court of Zimri-Lim. Despite the likelihood of this line of reasoning, the cirumstances surrounding Addu-Duri's coming to Mari remain obscure.[36]

Ama-dugga

Ama-dugga,[37] as has long been known, was a servant of Šamši-Adad who later passed into the service of Zimri-Lim.[38] She is known primarily from her seal, which identifies her as a servant of Šamši-Adad.[39] She evidently came to Mari with the Assyrian takeover. But as with some other Assyrian officials, Ama-dugga's talents were utilized by Zimri-Lim when he ousted Yasmaḫ-Addu. Although her function under Yasmaḫ-Addu is not known, under Zimri-Lim she seems to have served as supervisor of kitchen supplies. Her seal is imprinted on numerous oil receipts and on a few receipts for cereals. Nevertheless, her function is somewhat ambiguous. Apart from a single text, where she personally received a delivery of honey (XI 270), her name appears only in the seal impression. Normally the name of some other functionary who received the oil or grain appears in the text of the receipt itself. These officials were either Ilukanum, Ili-Ašraya, or Balumenuḫḫe. At least one of these functionaries, Ilukanum,[40] had his own seal; so why they used Ama-dugga's seal is yet to be explained. Perhaps they served under her and the stamp of her seal implied that these men were but her assistants and that responsibility for the accuracy of their work lay with Ama-dugga herself.

Conclusion

Although the women of this chapter provide interesting studies in themselves, few conclusions can be drawn because we do not know, for the most part, their titles, positions, and/or relationships to the royal family. Belassunu, as a visiting foreign princess, may be omitted from discussion here. Ama-dugga, the least important, may have been nothing more than the kitchen supervisor. Inibšina, the governor's wife, was possibly related to Zimri-Lim, though we make no such assumption. Addu-duri almost certainly was not a blood relative of the royal family. As a group these women illustrate that women in Mari could attain great power, often although not always unofficially, witness Addu-duri, the most prominent of them all, who seemingly held a position with some kind of recognized jurisdication. It is perhaps significant that they all flourished during the Zimri-Lim period; comparable examples from other periods are virtually nonexistent. Taking into account the varied backgrounds and widely differing functions of these women, perhaps the most one can say is that under Zimri-Lim, at least, it was possible for women to achieve distinction and power without necessarily belonging to the royal family.

NOTES TO CHAPTER 3

OTHER SERVANTS OF THE KING

[1]See below, chap. 4, pp. 86-87.

[2]See Kupper, "Baḫdi-Lim," 587, n. 5.

[3]Renger, *Priestertum* I, 146; Falkenstein, *apud* Renger, *Priestertum* I, 141, n. 223a; *CAD* E, 173.

[4]"Royal Ladies," 60-61.

[5]See Moran, *Biblica* 50 (1969), 33; we do not, of course, accept Moran's statement that this woman is Zimri-Lim's daughter and the *ugbabtum*.

[6]See above, chap. 1, p. 13.

[7]See below, chap. 9, p. 122.

[8]See above, chap. 1, p. 18-19.

[9]Presumably this is the same Inibšina "que les textes juridiques de Mari nous révèlent comme une active femme d'affaires, se livrant, sur les grains, à de vaste opérations commerciales," in the communiqué of G. Boyer reported by Birot, *RA* 50 (1956), 58, n. 2. If, however, this woman is the *ugbabtum*, then one should compare her activities with the secular activities of the *ugbabtum* in the Old Assyrian documents. Ištar-lamasi the *ugbabtum*, like most of the Assyrian colonists in Cappadocia, is actively engaged in commercial enterprises, particularly the clothing trade (*TC* III 128A; Bohl, Leiden 1201, with the corrections noted by J. Lewy, *Or* 15 [1946], 400, n. 7, and *ArOr* 18/3 [1950], 372); for further activities of this woman, see J. Lewy, *HUCA* 27 (1956), 79, n. 333.

[10]See above, chap. 1, p. 23.

[11]*JNES* 32 (1973), 340-41, and "Royal Ladies," 61-62.

[12]After S. Page, *Iraq* 30 (1968), 93f.

[13]S. Page, *Rencontre XVIIe*, 181.

[14]*Iraq* 30 (1968), 93f.; *Rencontre XVIIe*, 181.

[15]See TR 4212, as reported in *Iraq* 30 (1968), 94.

[16]Or *aq-bu-am-mu-ú-ma* ÌR!-*ki-ma* "Ḫaqba-Ḫammu, your servant."

[17]Huffmon, *APNM*, 35; XIII 36.28, 34; 37.11; X 73.30.

[18]See above, chap. 1, p. 11.

[19]See the contrary opinion of Birot, *ARMT* IX, 262.

[20]I follow the interpretation of Soden (*UF* 1, 198) and Berger (*UF* 1, 209), who restore line 29f. *šārti u sissikti s*[*inništim*(MI)] *aknukamma* "I sealed (and sent to my lord) the hem and lock of the woman." These symbols were not required for dreams. Therefore, the restoration of Moran (*Biblica* 50 [1969], 38, and cf. 20) and Ellermeier (*Prophetie*, 66) at the beginning of line 30, [*anāku*], "I myself seal my hem and lock...," is to be avoided.

[21]The *tulū* was evidently a part of the door; cf. 2 *tu-*[*l*]*i ša* GIŠ.GÁL.ḪI.A, *RA* 64 (1970), 21, 2.2 and see the editor's discussion on p. 41. Or should the word be connected with *tulū* "breast," here perhaps breastplates

for the statue of Annunitum?

[22]On Aḫum, the *šangûm* of the Annunitum temple, see below, chap. 9, p. 122.

[23]Perhaps instead of [š]a, one should read É, thus "the golden *tulû* of the house of Annunitum."

[24]*asallu* is doubly difficult; the present tense may represent the past durative (*GAG* #78c, d), while the subjunctive is perhaps to be explained after the fashion of Finet, *L'Accadien*, #91f-h.

[25]"Simaḫlânê, roi de Kurda," *RA* 66 (1972), 131-39.

[26]For this meaning of *ḫiṭītum*, see F. R. Kraus, *RA* 64 (1970), 53-55, who adduces this very text in support of his thesis.

[27]In this connection, one perhaps ought to adduce text VII 105, in which there is mention of the sacred property (*asakkum*) of Adad of Terqa(??). Addu-duri's name occurs on the reverse. However the broken condition of the tablet precludes determining Addu-duri's connection with the sacred property or even the purpose of the tablet.

[28]This may have been a West Semitic feast; see *AHw* 921 *qilā/ūṣātum*. In VII 263.i.7 the feast is said to be in honor of Itur-Mer (*qí-la-sa-tim ša* [d]*i-túr-me-er*); see further Bottéro, *ARMT* VII, 343; Burke, *ARMT* XI, 132-33.

[29]For Mukannišum's connection with female weavers, see above, chap. 1, p. 13, and below, chap. 4, p. 85.

[30]Addu-duri seems to have been similarly involved in the settlement of legal claims involving money in X 56 and 59. Both of these letters are poorly preserved, however, and Addu-duri's precise function in each case is obscured. In the latter text, there is mention of a *qadištum* of Annunitum; see below, chap. 7, p. 111. The *qadištum* appears to be subject to the authority of Addu-duri. Addu-duri's supervisory role over the temples and temple personnel has already been discussed above, pp. 65ff.

[31]*MAM* II, 227.

[32]The reading of this name is disputed. For the first element, I follow Huffmon, *APNM* 205-6; for the ambiguity of the sign AN, see *ibid*, 162-65. In the two writings of this PN which are definitely complete, the form is *ḫa-at-ni*-AN-*ma* (VI 38.13´; VIII 77.1). On Addu-duri's seal, as in II 45.6, the AN sign is followed by a break and may be incomplete. None of these PNs unequivocally ends with the AN sign.

[33]A glance at the photographs of Addu-duri's seal impressions, *MAM* II, 191, fig. 109, and pl. XLVII, #227, shows that the imprint is barely complete at the beginning and broken at the end. The AN sign in the second register is certainly followed by another sign now lost in the break.

[34]Kupper, *RA* 53 (1959), 99. This is perhaps the same Ḫatni-Addu who had three daughters (A.4634.8; see *RA* 64 [1970], 43). The PNs in this text are ill-attested at Mari and are perhaps all kings and their daughters.

[35]See above, chap. 1, p. 9.

[36]After this study was completed the writer came upon Finet's hypothesis (*Rencontre XVIII*, 69; see above chap. 2, n. 39) that Addu-duri was Šibtu's replacement as queen after the death of the latter. While this

hypothesis would readily account for most of the evidence regarding Addu-duri, it should be noted that there is no direct evidence either for Šibtu's death or for Addu-duri as a wife of Zimri-Lim.

[37]Perhaps the Sumerian name AMA-DÙG-GA is to be given its Akkadian equivalent Ummi-ṭaba. The Akkadian name was a frequent one at Mari: IX 291. i.31; 24.iii.17; XIII 1.v.2; viii.39; xiii.24; xiv.27.

[38]See Birot, *ARMT* IX, 251; XII, 19.

[39]For a possible second seal of Ama-dugga which bears the title "Servant of Zimri-Lim," see Birot, *ARMT* XII, 19, n. 1.

[40]Ilukanum had two seals. The imprint of the first appears on VII 155. The imprint of his second seal appears on XI 12; 32 *et passim*; see also *MAM* II, 255.

PART II

WOMEN IN RELIGION

CHAPTER 4

THE *UGBABTUM* PRIESTESS

Despite her high rank, Mesopotamian sources tell us little about the function of the *ugbabtum*.[1] Her role is further obscured by the ambiguity of the sumerogram NIN.DINGIR, which is used for both the *ugbabtum* and the *entum* priestesses.[2] Because neither *entum* nor *ugbabtum* are syllabically spelled, except in rare instances,[3] it can be difficult to decide which of the two priestesses is meant in a given case. It is generally assumed that *ugbabtum* is meant when the reference is to a priestess of less than the highest social rank or when more than one NIN.DINGIR is mentioned in the same text.[4]

Normally, the *ugbabtum* lived in a cloister, although she might live in the house of her father. Many of the same rules which governed the life of the *nadītum* applied to the *ugbabtum* as well. The *ugbabtum* was not permitted to marry or to bear children. She was of higher rank than the *nadītum* but lower than the *entum* priestess. She might, however, be elevated to the rank of *entum* upon the death of the latter. The *ugbabtum*'s role in the cult is not yet defined.[5]

The Mari evidence may be grouped into three categories: (1) the *ugbabtum* of Dagan in Terqa and matters pertaining to her house, (2) the *ugbabātum*[6] (NIN.DINGIR.RA.MEŠ) of Adad of Kulmiš, and (3) *ugbabātum* mentioned by name. Each of these categories will be examined in turn.

For knowledge of the first, the *ugbabtum* of Dagan in Terqa, we are dependent upon three letters of Kibri-Dagan, the governor of Terqa.[7] The background for this correspondence is only alluded to, a mere reference to the "house of the previous *ugbabtum*" (É [f]*ug-ba-ab-tim pa-ni-tim*, III 42.12; 84.5), which Kibri-Dagan is now (re-)building. As Renger[8] has observed, this "house of the previous *ugbabtum*" dates to the Assyrian interregnum. The Assyrian dynasty seems to have originated in Terqa, and the devotion of Šamši-Adad and his sons to Dagan of Terqa is well attested.[9] In the period of transfer of power from the Assyrian to the local dynast Zimri-Lim, the dwelling of the *ugbabtum* must have fallen into a state of disrepair. To judge from the sequel, even the office of *ugbabtum* was vacated. After having solidified his control over the throne of Mari, Zimri-Lim--whose own piety toward Dagan is much in evidence,[10] as was that of his father Yaḫdun-Lim[11]--set about rectifying this neglect, restoring the residence of the *ugbabtum* and appointing another priestess.

In the (chronologically) first of Kibri-Dagan's letters, he states that he is undertaking this restoration at the direction of Zimri-Lim, "in accordance with what my lord wrote me previously, concerning the house in which the *ugbabtum* of Dagan is to live..." (III 42.7-10). Kibri-Dagan writes that he has had omens taken and that they were favorable. Accordingly, he has started "to put that building in order and to oversee (the repair of) its chinks (in the wall)."[12]

But in a second letter Kibri-Dagan has cause for reservation. The letter is not entirely legible, but it appears that since the report given in the last letter certain difficulties have appeared. The question has come up whether this dwelling was proper for an *ugbabtum* (III 84.10 and 20f.). The objections are twofold. The nature of the first is difficult to determine.[13] The second[14] objection was to the possibility that the residence of the priestess would be too close to that of a woman who made *mirsum*-pastries.[15] Apparently, *ugbabātum* had to maintain a certain dignity, perhaps even a certain distance from profane activities. This is manifest not only in CH #110, forbidding the *ugbabtum* to enter a tavern, but also in the fact that *ugbabātum* as a role resided in cloisters. The *ugbabtum*'s house here is apparently viewed as a quasi-cloister. Accordingly, Kibri-Dagan writes that he has again had omens taken about the matter and that this time the god gave his approval: "he (the god) is in complete accord over the dwelling-place of the *ugbabtum*" (*šu-ú a-na wa-ša-ab* ᶠ*ug-ba-ab-tim* [*k*]*a-la-šu du-um-mu-uq*, 11.26-27).[16] Nevertheless, Kibri-Dagan still has reservations and so asks the king to advise him further.

The outcome must have been that the house was indeed completed, for in the third letter there is the question of bringing the *ugbabtum* to Terqa, undoubtedly to live in the newly restored residence. The king had written to Kibri-Dagan to come to Mari apparently to escort the young *ugbabtum*[17] back to Terqa. Kibri-Dagan excuses himself from coming because of the urgency of a project in which he is currently engaged. Instead, he urges the king himself to escort the girl to Terqa, "May my lord, out of the goodness of his heart, come up and himself kiss the feet of Dagan, the one who loves him! (Meanwhile) I will complete the work (here). I cannot possibly come!"

In this series of letters the *ugbabtum* of Dagan seems to be the equivalent of the *entum* priestess in Babylonia proper, that is, a single high priestess dedicated to the service of the principal god of a region. The *entum* does not seem to be attested at Mari. Dagan, although one of the most important West Semitic gods and the principal god of Terqa and the middle Euphrates region, is not one of the "great" gods of the Sumerian tradition, a fact which may explain why this god's priestess was an *ugbabtum* and not an *entum*. Bottéro[19] draws the connection with the *entum* even closer by comparing the "house" of this *ugbabtum* to the *gipārum* of the high preistess.

The second group of texts yields a somewhat different situation. A different god is involved, Adad of Kulmiš, and in this case there are a number of *ugbabātum*[20] associated with him, the exact number being unknown.[21] The location of Kulmiš is not known and is, so far as I know, attested only in these texts.[22] However, the unique feature of these *ugbabātum* of Adad of Kulmiš is their manner of "recruitment."

Because of its crucial importance, X 123 will be quoted at length:

a-na ^{f}*ši-i[b-tu]*
qí-bí-ma
um-ma be-el-ki-ma
as-su-ur-ri mi-im-ma ṭe$_4$*-ma-am*
te-še-em-me-e-ma li-ib-ba-ki
i-na-aḫ-ḫi-id mi-im-[m]a LÚ.KÚR *a-na* GIŠ.TUKUL
a-na pa-ni-ia ú-ul ip-ti-na-am
[š]u-⸢ul⸣-mu-um mi-im-ma li-ib-ba-ki
[la i-na]-aḫ-ḫi-id
⸢*ú*(?)⸣ ^{d}IM *ša kúl-mi-iš*
[aš-]šum NIN.DINGIR.RA.MEŠ-*šu-ma*
[da-]li-iḫ-tam an-ni-tam id-lu-uḫ
[i-n]a tup-pí ša-al-la-tim ša ú-ša-re-e-em

[NI]N.DINGIR.RA.MEŠ *ša kúl-mi-iš*
⌜*ù*⌝ NIN.DINGIR.RA.MEŠ *ša* DINGIR.MEŠ
⌜*a-ḫu*⌝*-ne-e i-na tup-pí-im i-di-ša-am šu-uṭ-ṭú-ra*
⌜*i*⌝*-na-an-na* NIN.DINGIR.RA.MEŠ *ša kúl-mi-iš-ma*
a-na ra-ma-ni-ši-na a-na [*at?-lu?-ki?-im?*]
li-bi-ru TÚG.ḪI.A *lu-ub-bi̭-ši-ši-na-ti-ma*
i-na x x x x *ša* 2 ^{gis}*ma-ga-ar-ru-ša*
ù [ ]x *da? ši*
li-š[*a-ar?-ki?-bu?-ši-n*]*a-ti-ma*
LÚ.TUR.MEŠ *ša iš-tu an-na-nu-um-ma*
ir-du-ši-na-t[*i*] *a-na ṣe-ri-ia*
li-ša-a[*l-li-mu-nim*]
ù iš-te[*-et la* ...]

To Šibtu, say, thus (says) your lord: Perhaps you have heard some rumor and have become alarmed. No armed enemy has withstood me! All is well; there is no reason for you to be alarmed. Now Adad of Kulmiš has caused this disturbance because of his *ugbabātum*! In the tablet of the prisoners-of-war which I sent, the *ugbabātum* of (Adad of) Kulmiš and the *ugbabātum* of the (other) gods were separately listed, each one individually, in (that) tablet. Now then, let them pick out the *ugbabātum* of (Adad of) Kulmiš by themselves (i.e., as a separate group) for [...]. You clothe them with garments. Then they shall put them aboard(?) two-wheeled wagons(?) and.....Let the servants who brought them from here now conduct them back safely to me; [not] a single one of them [is to be injured(?)].[23]

Apparently Zimri-Lim had suffered minor reverses in his campaign in the field, for his assurances to his queen and wife that there is really nothing to worry about appear to be a tacit admission that something has gone awry. Although there is no necessary connection between Zimri-Lim's troubles in the field and the following *ugbabātum* incident, I think that they were connected in the mind of Zimri-Lim. Unless "*this* disturbance" (line 12) harkens back to some incident reported by Šibtu in an unpreserved letter to the king, then "*this* disturbance" does refer to Zimri-

Lim's reverses alluded to in the preceding lines. If this is the case, then the king believes that his reverses are due to the displeasure of Adad, apparently because of some grievance on the part of the priestesses of this god, the nature of which will be investigated shortly.

The startling feature of this letter, however, is the revelation that these *ugbabātum* were acquired as prisoners-of-war (*šallatum*).[24] Were these *ugbabātum* in the service of Adad at a place named Kulmiš when they were captured, or were they assigned to the service of Adad of Kulmiš after they were captured? Our interpretation of the text would allow only the former possibility. This conclusion seems inescapable because of other letters which group the *ugbabātum* together with female weavers (*išparātum*). In a letter to Šibtu, Zimri-Lim writes:

> [*a-n*]*u-um-ma* ^f^UŠ.BAR.MEŠ *uš-ta-ri-ki-im*
> [*i-n*]*a li-ib-bi-ši-na* NIN.DINGIR.RA.MEŠ
> [*i-b*]*a-aš-še-e* NIN.DINGIR.RA.MEŠ *bi-ri-ma*
> *a-na* É ^f^UŠ.BAR.MEŠ *pí-iq-di-ši-na-ti*
>
> Now I have sent you some female weavers; there are some *ugbabātum* among them. Pick out the *ugbabātum* and assign the others (lit., them) to the textile factory (X 126.4-7).

It is not explicitly stated that the *ugbabātum* of Adad of Kulmiš were among this group, but it seems very likely that such is the case. The women that the king is sending were all taken as war booty (*šallatum*), as a comparison with X 125 makes clear:

> *a-na* ^f^*ši-ib-tu*
> *qí-bí-ma*
> *um-ma be-el-ki-i-ma*
> *aš-šum* SAL.TUR.MEŠ *ši-it-ri-im*
> *i-na ša-al-la-tim ša ú-ša-re-em*
> *bi-ri-im ša i-na pa-ni-tim*
> *aš-pu-ra-am*[*-ma*]
> *i-na-an-na mi*[*-im-ma*]
> *i-na ša-al-la-t*[*im*] *ša-a-t*[*i*]
> SAL.TUR.MEŠ *ši-it-ra-am*
> *la i-bi-ir-ru*
> SAL.TUR.MEŠ *ši-na*

a-na ^{f}UŠ.BAR-*tim-ma*
li-in-na-de-e
ša-al-la-tum a-na pa-ni-ia
ib-ba-aš-ši
a-na-ku-ma i-na ša-al-la-tim
ša ib-ba-aš-šu-ú
SAL.TUR.MEŠ *a-na ši-it-ri-im*
e-bi-ir-ra-am-ma
ú-ša-ra-am

To Šibtu say, thus (says) your lord: Concerning what I previously wrote you, (namely) the selection of girls for the veil from among the booty which I have sent--now then, they are not to select any girls for the veil from among that booty. (Rather) let those girls be set aside as female weavers. There is (other) booty here before me; I myself will select girls for the veil from among the booty which is here and I will send (them to you).

Letters X 125 and X 126 are readily seen to overlap in subject matter,[25] and in X 125.5, 9, and 17 these women are explicitly said to be war booty. Consequently, if the *ugbabātum* of X 126 are war booty, it seems impossible not to connect them with the *ugbabātum* of Adad of Kulmiš spoken of in X 123.

Thus the historical situation may be reconstructed approximately as follows. These *ugbabātum* were in the service of Adad at some place named Kulmiš. Zimri-Lim apparently captured Kulmiš at the same time as Ašlakka.[26] The victorious monarch then took many women captive and shipped them back to Mari as slaves to work in the textile factory. The textile industry in the OB period appears to have been, at least at Mari, a royal monopoly, and large amounts of slave labor would have been needed to staff it. Dossin is certainly correct in assuming that the long fourteen column tablet (XIII 1) of female weavers is a list of captured women engaged in the royal textile factory.[27] Whether this list represents the total number of women so engaged, or only those captured at the time when Ašlakka was conquered, is not known.

Among the women captured at this time and sent to Mari were the *ugbabātum* from the local shrine of Adad at Kulmiš, together with a number of other *ugbabātum* in the service of other gods. These priestesses were spared the indignity of being assigned to the textile factory. But the matter did not end there. The *ugbabātum* of Kulmiš were evidently superior to the other *ugbabātum*, probably because of the superior rank of the god to whom they were dedicated. This distinction was originally recognized (X 123.13-16) but was later disregarded (X 126.4-7), thus inflicting humiliation upon them. Subsequently, when Zimri-Lim suffered some reverses in his campaign, he surmised the cause to be this humiliating treatment of the priestesses of Adad of Kulmiš (X 126). How Zimri-Lim arrived at this conclusion is unknown. At any rate, he then commanded that these *ugbabātum* be sent back to him (at Kulmiš ?). We are left with the impression that they were perhaps to be reinstated in their old capacity.

Two further texts are connected with this incident. One is so broken that it only preserves a mention of the *ugbabātum*: NIN.DINGIR.RA.MEŠ *ša* ^{d}IM *ša kúl-mi-iš* (VI 46.4). The other (XIII 21), also broken, is more legible. This letter is written to the king by Mukannišum, who is one of the very officials who, according to X 126.25f., was to take charge of these weavers.[28] The reverse side of the tablet seems to contain Mukannišum's response to Zimri-Lim's instructions. For we are dealing again with war booty (line 3´), mostly women. Most, if not all, of these female war-booty slaves are said to have been introduced into the "house of female weavers" (lines 9´ and 12´). The remainder of the tablet is badly broken, but in view of the volume X texts already quoted, a better restoration of the following lines might be suggested:

[*ša-ni-tam* N]IN.DINGIR.RA.MEŠ
[*sa* (^{d}IM *ša*) *kúl-mi*]-*iš*
15´) [*a-na-ku a-na ṣ*]*e-er be-lí-ia*
[*a-ṭà-ra-da*]-*am*

In addition, *I am sending* (back)[29] to my lord the *ugbabātum* (of Adad) of Kulmiš.[30]

If my restoration is correct, this text is a statement that the king's orders are being carried out. The final resolution of the case is not known.

Returning to "the *ugbabātum* of the (other) gods" (X 123.15-16), we may conclude that this group of priestesses were left in Mari. They were not treated like other women captives, who were forced to work in the textile factories. In fact the din and bustle from the textile workshops appear to have been considered unbecoming for an *ugbabtum*, for the proximity of MÍ.MEŠ *iš-*[*pa-*]*ra-*[*tum*] LÚ.MEŠ.TÚG *ù* DUMU.MEŠ *um-me-ni* "female weavers,[31] fullers,[32] and artisans" (III 84.11-12) evidently constituted the first objection to the proposed location of the dwelling for the *ugbabtum* of Dagan in Terqa.[33] The dignity of the *ugbabātum* was maintained even in captivity. But just what their duties were remains unknown.

Turning now to other *ugbabātum*, we find that several are known to us by name. Foremost among these is Inibšina, who is identified as an *ugbabtum* of Adad[34] and also as a king's daughter.[35] But which king's daughter? Since at least some of the other eight women in this same text who are likewise designated as king's daughters are known to have been daughters of Zimri-Lim, Moran assumed that Inibšina was also a daughter of Zimri-Lim.[36] Other scholars have been more cautious.[37] Yaḫdun-Lim evidently also had a daughter who was a priestess and whose name seems to have been Inibšina.[38] Despite the fact that Zimri-Lim is known to have dedicated an unnamed daughter to the service of Adad of Appan,[39] this writer is inclined to equate Inibšina *ugbabtum* of Adad with the priestess-daughter of Yaḫdun-Lim. The homonymous Inibšina, the governor's wife, is of course to be completely disassociated from the *ugbabtum*.[40]

There is, then, no unequivocal evidence that Inibšina, the *ugbabtum* of Adad, was a daughter of Zimri-Lim. In fact, the evidence could indicate that she was a daughter of Yaḫdun-Lim. The reason why she heads the list of "king's daughters" (C i.4) could be as much her age (she would be the aunt of Zimri-Lim's daughters) as her rank as an *ugbabtum*. Similarly, the reason why Inibšina precedes queen Šibtu and other royal ladies (VII 206.4′) could be explained by her rank both as a princess (and the sister of Zimri-Lim) and as an *ugbabtum*. This is the same *Inib-*[*šina*] *mārat Yaḫdu*[*n-Lim*] *amtum ša* ^{d}[ ] who elsewhere also received a ration of ghee for ointment (XI 191).[41]

Since Inibšina has left no correspondence,[42] virtually nothing can be said of the function of this *ugbabtum*. She was supported out of the royal stores: with choice cuts of meat, always a luxury, VII 206.4′ (2 [*m*]*a-la-ku*); with oil, C i.4; XI 191;[43] with garments, VII 220.1; and with money, VII 139.1.[44]

Other *ugbabātum* are mentioned by name in the Mari documents. Tašuba, the *ugbabtum* (= NIN.DINGIR.RA) is listed among those bringing a sheep as a gift to the palace (VII 225.10′ = 226.50). We know nothing more about this priestess. She perhaps also resided at Mari. One largely illegible text contains the names of two additional *ugbabātum*: *pa-an* ^{f}*um-mi-ia ù* ^{f}x[ ] *ug-ba-ba-tum li*-x[ ] "Let...before Ummiya and [PN], the *ugbabātum*" (X 170.9-11). Since the writer of this letter, Ibal-Addu, is the king of Ašlakka, we may speculate that these last two priestesses are from that city and both once functioned there. It is not impossible that these two *ugbabātum* were among those female captives from the region of Ašlakka referred to in X 123.[46] Because of Ibal-Addu's personal interest in them, one may even speculate that these two women were blood relations of the king of Ašlakka, perhaps even princesses. This would be but one more indication of the prestigious rank of the *ugbabtum* in northern Mesopotamia.

Conclusion

In general the Mari materials concerning the *ugbabtum* agree with what is known of this priestess from elsewhere. She was of high social status and apparently not married. Knowledge of her cultic function remains vague. At Terqa there appears to have been only one *ugbabtum*--at least in the service of Dagan. At other places, however, more than one *ugbabtum* served the same deity at the same time.[46]

Compared with *ugbabātum* in southern Mesopotamia, the rank of the *ugbabtum* in the Mari region is ambiguous; the term *ugbabtum* is used for both high-ranking and seemingly low-ranking priestesses. On the one hand, in some of the Mari texts, the *ugbabtum* seems to be the highest-ranking priestess; this conclusion is supported by the lack of evidence for the existence of either the *en* or the *entum* priestesses. Furthermore, whenever the evidence is explicit, the *ugbabātum* of the Mari tablets serve the principal deities of the region: Dagan in Terqa, Adad of Kulmiš, or simply Adad (in Mari?). Other deities also had their *ugbabātum*, although they are not specified by name. The prominence of Inibšina the princess among the ranks of the *ugbabātum* convinces us that the *ugbabtum* was indeed the highest-ranking priestess at Mari. On the other hand, other texts speak of a multiplicity of *ugbabātum* and convey the impression that some of them are not of particularly high origin or status. It may be that at Mari the word *ugbabtum* is the general word for "priestess" and thus could encompass different types of priestesses.

NOTES TO CHAPTER 4

THE *UGBABTUM* PRIESTESS

[1]For the latest treatment of the *ugbabtum*, see Renger, *Priestertum* I, 144-49. The Old Assyrian materials have been reviewed by Hirsch, *Untersuchungen zur altassyrischen Religion* (Graz, 1961), 56-57.

[2]For the equation NIN.DINGIR = *ugbabtum*, see Renger, *Priestertum* I, 144-49.

[3]For the attested syllabic writings of *ugbabtum*, see *ibid.*, p. 144, n. 240, and p. 148, n. 263 (with the correction: Lewy, *ArOr* 18/3, 342, n. 37). Renger has failed to cite the unusual Assyrian spelling *ug-ba-áb-tim* (*TC* III 128 B: 1), along with the usual Assyrian spelling *gu$_5$-ba-áb-tu/im*.

[4]See *CAD* E, 173; similarly, Renger, *Priestertum* I, 134f.

[5]*Ibid.*, pp. 146f.

[6]The expected plural *ugbabātum* is now attested: *ug-ba-ba-tim* (X 170.11). Previously, only the abnormal *ú-ug-ba-ak-ka-ti* (*CT* 46 3 vii 6 = Atraḫasis) was known.

[7]III 8; 42; 84.

[8]*Priestertum* I, 147.

[9]See Hallo and Simpson, *The Ancient Near East* (New York, 1971), 96-97. Šamši-Adad and his sons for the temple of Dagan, naming one of the years of his reign after this event, see Dossin, *SM*, 53, year no. 1. The concern of Šamši-Adad and his sons for the temple of Dagan is further exemplified in I 74.35f.; II 15.39f.; IV 72.31f.

[10]Some of Zimri-Lim's more important activities toward Dagan include erecting a large statue for Dagan in Terqa (year no. 14 [cf. year no. 15, *SM*, 56; and also XIII 5.5; 110.5f.; 47]); installing lions at the entrance of the Dagan temple in Mari (year no. 25, *SM*, 58); and presenting a ceremonial weapon to Dagan (*Syria* 20, 107). For Dagan as a patron deity of Zimri-Lim, see the latter's seal: *Zimrī-Lim / šakin* *ᵈDagan*, etc. (see *ARMT* IX, 250; cf. *SM*, 42); Dagan is called "your (Zimri-Lim) lord" (X 62.14-5; 100.7); Dagan delivers oracles in favor of Zimri-Lim (II 90.17f.; XIII 23; 114; *RA* 42, 125f.). For cult and sacrifice in the time of Zimri-Lim in honor of Dagan, see VII 263.ii.12; IX 191.3; XIII 23; *SM*, 43f.; V 79; VI 73.

[11]See Yahdun-Lim's disk-foundation inscription: *ᵈda-gan / šar-ru-ti ib-bi* "Dagan proclaimed my kingship," *RA* 33 (1936), 49f., col. i, 9-10.

[12]The proposal to see in *mi-ir*-KI-*ti-šu* a reference to the secluded quarters ("claustrum") of the residence of the *ugbabtum*, so Oppenheim, *JNES* 11 (1952), 138-39, followed by *CAD* Ḫ, 160 ("hidden chambers"), is not justified philologically. See now *AHw* 658, s.v. *miriqtu(m)* "schadhafte Stelle (in Mauern)," citing this passage, "*mi-ir-qê-ti-šu* zu prüfen."

[13]See below, p. 86.

[14]Instead of the editor's [*an*]-*ni-tam*, one should restore [*ša*]-*ni-tam ni-iš-ta-a*[*l-ma*] "Again we consulted..." or, perhaps more likely, "We consulted (on the) second matter (or omen)." Cf. X 55.19-20: ⸢*i*⸣-[*na*] *ša-ni-tim a-ša-al-lu* "I inquired with a second (omen)"; and see above, chap. 3, p. 67, with n. 24.

[15]*a-na ki-sa-al* É.GAL-*lim qé-er-bi-*[*it*] [*š*]*a a-ša-ar* ^{f}*ku-un-du-la-tum e-pí-ša-at mi-ir-si-im wa-aš-ba-at* (III 84.21f.).

[16]For this reading, see Falkenstein, *BiOr* 11 (1954), 117. Or perhaps read [*d*]*u'-la-šu* "his work is all right," with von Soden, *Or* 21 (1952), 86. Kupper's [*q*]*u(?)-la-šu* "sa voix (?)" is untenable for both lexical and contextual reasons.

[17]*aš-šum a-la-ki-ia a-na ma-ri*^{ki} *a-na pa-an* SAL.TUR *ug-ba-ab-tim be-lí iš-pu-ra-am* (III 8.5-7).

[18]See Renger, *Priestertum* I, 147-48.

[19]*La femme*, 218.

[20]For the *ugbabātum* of Adad of Kulmiš the sumerogram NIN.DINGIR.RA.MEŠ is always used, whereas for the priestess of Dagan of Terqa, *ugbabtum* is written syllabically, a fact that seems to be without significance. The writing NIN.DINGIR.RA at Mari (versus the normal NIN.DINGIR) is an incorporation of the Sumerian genitive element into the sumerogram; see Renger, *Priestertum* I, 148, n. 261, and 135, n. 167, for occurrences of this writing elsewhere.

[21]The texts in question are VI 46; X 123; 126; XIII 21.

[22]Kulmiš may have been part of or at least located near Ašlakka. X 123.23f. seems to imply that the *ugbabātum* of Kulmiš are from the same locale from which Zimri-Lim dispatches his letter. The reference to the daughter of Ibal-Addu (line 27) suggests that Zimri-Lim is writing from Ašlakka, since Ibal-Addu is king of that city; see below, chap. 6, p. 109. Indeed, it is not impossible that some of the *ugbabātum* referred to in X 123 are from the city of Ašlakka and mentioned by name in X 170.9-11; see below, p. 87.

[23]The reading of line 26 was suggested to me by Moran.

[24]The *kezertum* was also acquired as war booty; see below, chap. 8, pp. 115-116.

[25]See above, chap. 1, pp. 26-27, where text X 126 is given in full; see also p. 13.

[26]See above, n. 22.

[27]Dossin, *Syria* 41 (1964), 21-24.

[28]Mukannišum's activities include the overseeing of many different kinds of artisans; see Bottéro *ARMT* XIII, 17. He is specifically mentioned as one of those in charge of the female weavers in XIII 1.xiv.65. See further Sasson, *Iraq* 34 (1972), 59-60.

[29]The verb *ṭarādum* is more commonly used with persons and is thus to be preferred to the editor's *šūbulum*.

[30]In view of the context, the editor's restoration, [*ar-ḫi*]-*iš*, is most unlikely. The lack of a copy of the text makes it difficult to decide whether to restore the longer form including the god's name or the abbreviated form: [*ša kúl-mi*]-*iš*.

[31]Oppenheim, *JNES* 11 (1952), 139, wished to read *iš*-[*t*]*a-ra*-[*tum*] here, followed by *CAD* I, 271 and *AHw* 399: *iš-t*[*a-r*]*e*-[*e-tum*]; Renger, *Priestertum* I, 184, n. 534, has correctly recognized that one must read *iš*-[*pa-*] *ra*-[*tum*] because of the following male workers.

[32]There is no need to posit here an otherwise unattested "forme abrégée de l'idéogramme ḪUN.GA = *agrum* 'mercenaire,' 'journalier,'" as does the editor, *ARMT* III, 118, followed by *CAD* I, 271; Renger, *Priestertum* I, 184, n. 534. The presence of *išparātum* makes it obvious that the ideogram is simply LÚ.MEŠ.TÚG; for the positioning of MEŠ at Mari, see *ARMT* XV, 89, n. 4.

[33]See above, p. 80.

[34]1 1/2 SILA (Ì.BA) *i-ni-ib-ši-na* NIN.DINGIR.RA ᵈIM (C i.4-5 = *RA* 50 [1956], 68). In view of the constant writing of the sumerogram at Mari, *Biblica* 50 (1969), 33, is correct in reading here NIN.DINGIR.RA ᵈIŠKUR instead of the editor's NIN.DINGIR *ša* ᵈ*Addu*.

[35]C i.17.

[36]Moran, *Biblica* 50 (1969), 33.

[37]Birot, *RA* 50 (1956), 58, n. 2; Renger, *Priestertum* I, 148, n. 262. Sasson, "Royal Ladies," 60, also argues for the identity of Inibšina the *ugbabtum* with the daughter of Yaḫdun-Lim, while interpreting other pertinent evidence differently from this writer.

[38]Three seal impressions, all broken and all from Room 79, yield the composite reading: ᶠ*Inib*-[ ] *mārat Yaḫdu*[*n-Lim*] *amtum ša* ᵈ[x]; see XI 191 seal, and see Birot *apud* Burke, *ARMT* XI, 127; Birot *apud* Renger, *Priestertum* I, 148, n.262.

The possibility, mentioned by Birot, that Inib-šarri should be restored here can now confidently be ruled out, since the letters of Inib-šarri in volume X show that the only woman known by this name at Mari was the daughter of Zimri-Lim; see above, chap. 2, p. 37. The only other PNF thus far attested at Mari which begins with the element *Inib-* is Inib-Šamaš, the author of X 175, but she is hardly a candidate for the role under consideration here. Barring the unlikely possibility that we have here the name of an otherwise unattested princess, it is thus practically certain that Yaḫdun-Lim's daughter was named Inibšina.

The evidence for positing that Inibšina, the daughter of Yaḫdun-Lim is a priestess is not as certain as one would like. Birot and Renger understand the inscription on her seal *amtum ša* AN[ ] as evidence for her priesthood; the pattern of seal inscriptions from Mari may support this conclusion, despite the fact that ÌR DN in Babylonia commonly means "worshipper of DN." In addition, if our thesis that *Inibšina* NIN.DINGIR.RA ᵈIŠKUR, *mārat šarrim*, is not a daughter of Zimri-Lim should prove correct, then it would be extremely likely that this Inibšina is identical with the daughter of Yaḫdun-Lim known from the broken seal impressions.

[39]*šanat Zimrī-Lim mārtam ana* ᵈ*Addu ša Appān*ᵏⁱ *išlû* "The year in which Zimri-Lim sent(?) his daughter to Adad of Appan," year no. 23, *SM*, 58; cf. also year no. 24. For the verb *šalû* = Hebrew *šlḥ* "to send," see Dossin, *SM*, 58, n. 11.

[40]See above, chap. 3, pp. 59-61.

[41]See further Birot *apud* Renger, *Priestertum* I, 148, n. 262. The person whose name appears on the seal is the recipient of the goods named in the tablet, Bottéro, *ARMT* VII, 222, and Burke, *ARMT* XI, 125-27, 135, contrary to the statement of Sasson, "Royal Ladies," 60-61, that Inibšina is the dispenser of the ghee.

[42]See above, chap. 3, p. 60.

[43]See also Birot, *apud* Renger, *Priestertum* I, 148, n. 262, for notice of additional receipts of oil by Inibšina.

[44]Baḫlatum, who is linked with Inibšina in VII 139.1-2 and 206.4´-5´, is hardly an *ugbabtum*, as suggested by Bottéro (*ARMT* VII, 240), unless there is more than one noble lady by this name at Mari. Baḫlatum was married to Yasim-Dagan (X 173) and author of X 109; see Sasson, "Royal Ladies," 74-75.

[45]See above, p. 81, and n. 22.

[46]Renger, *Priestertum* I, 146-47, has assembled evidence to show that it is the normal situation to have more than one *ugbabtum* at the same time in the same locale. However, he himself admits that the Old Assyrian texts imply a situation in which but a single *ugbabtum*/*gubabtum* is assumed (*ibid*., 149).

CHAPTER 5

ERIŠTI-AYA, A *NADĪTUM*

The word *nadītum*[1] is thus far but rarely attested in the Mari texts,[2] nevertheless we do have considerable documentation from Mari about the role of one such woman. Although it is nowhere explicitly stated, it can be shown that Erišti-Aya, the author of eight letters (X 36-43), was a *nadītum* dedicated to the god Šamaš and his consort Aya. The following investigation will of necessity be limited to this one woman and her function as it can be ascertained from the Mari texts. For the *nadītum* in general, the reader is referred to the studies cited in note 1.

Erišti-Aya was the daughter of Zimri-Lim. Only in one place does she address him as *abiya* "my father" (X 42.1-2);[3] however, she normally does address him as "my Star" (*kakkabiya*), a term of respectful familiarity given the king and reserved, it seems, to members of the royal family.[4] Her mother was undoubtedly Šibtu, Zimri-Lim's chief wife and queen, for one of her letters is addressed *ana beltum*(sic!) *ummiya* "to the queen,[5] my mother" (X 42.1f.).

That Erišti-Aya was a *nadītum* is evident from a number of considerations. Her name, Erišti-Aya "Request from Aya," is one commonly given to *nadiātum*[6] and expresses her dedication to her mistress, the goddess Aya. The invocatory greetings with which Erišti-Aya begins her letters also reveal her to be a *nadītum*. The letters of *nadiātum* of Sippar customarily begin with the stereotyped salutation: *bēlī u bēltī liballiṭūka*, or in a more expanded form, *bēlī u bēltī aššumiya dāriš ūmī liballiṭūka* "May my lord and my lady preserve your life (permanently for my sake)!" There may be minor variations in the formula, but in general it was the hallmark of a letter written by a *nadītum*, so much so that it may often serve as the criterion for ascribing a given letter to a *nadītum*.[7] Erišti-Aya likewise begins her letters with an invocatory greeting which closely resembles that used at Sippar: *be-lí ù be-el-ti aš-šu-mi-ia li-ba-li-ṭú-ka* (X 40.4-6; 43. 5-6; cf. 42.5f.(?)). In one letter a little used variant, *mādiš ūmī* for *dāriš ūmī*, creeps into this salutation (X 38.5).[8] However, Erišti-Aya also employs another formula which was completely unknown at Sippar: *be-lí ù be-el-ti aš-šu-mi-ia ki-ma ša-me-e ù er-ṣi-tim li-ṣú-ru-ú-ka* "May my lord and my lady, for my sake, guard you like the heavens and the earth!" (X 36.4-7; 37.4-6; 41.4f.(?)). This eliptical formulation does not seem to be elsewhere attested;[9] however, it is little more than a variant of the fuller formula, "May my lord be everlasting as the heavens and the earth are everlasting" (*kīma šamû u erṣetum dārû lu dāri*).[10]

Another indication that Erišti-Aya was a *nadītum* comes from her statement that she is the king's special "emblem" who habitually prays for him in Šamaš's temple, Ebabbar (X 38.9-11). Further, Erišti-Aya states that she entered the cloister (*gagûm*, X 43.16).[11] Although other types of religious women did live in cloisters,[12] there can be no doubt that in this case the subject is a *nadītum*.

There are multiple indications throughout her letters that this Mari princess was not residing in her native city at the time of writing. As will be seen below, Erišti-Aya felt quite isolated and removed from the court of her father. This is hardly to be accounted for solely by the fact that she lived in a cloister. The *nadītum* was not nearly so sequestered as, for example, the medieval cloistered nun. A *nadītum* was allowed to leave the cloister to visit her relatives and also to have her relatives visit her.[13] Erišti-Aya's feeling of estrangement is best accounted for by supposing that her cloister was located at some distance from the court of her father, thus making visiting virtually impossible.

Important evidence on the location of Erišti-Aya's cloister is contained in the incidental remark made in a letter to her father. She states that her father has sent certain items which she has in turn offered to the goddess Aya, her "mistress," the "official in charge of foreigners" being her witness (*maḫar sukkal ubarē*) (X 38.23). The *sukkal ubarē* is known in the OB period,[14] although it is not previously attested as one of the officials found in a cloister. Since he is the sole witness invoked, it may fairly be supposed he was Erišti-Aya's superior. Erišti-Aya would thus be one of the *ubarē* "foreigners" and hence not native to the city in which she was residing. Her native city of Mari--and perhaps any city within the realm of Mari--is thus excluded.

It is known that not all of the *nadiātum* who inhabited a particular cloister were natives of that city. The most famous cases are the daughters of the kings of Babylon who became *nadiātum* in Sippar.[15] But there must have been many others[16] to warrant having an "official in charge of foreigners" as one of the officials of a cloister.

The most telling evidence against Erišti-Aya's residing in Mari is contained in her statement that she prays for her father in Ebabbar (X 38. 10), which is the name of a temple of Šamaš. The most famous such temple was located in Sippar. However, many cities had temples dedicated to Šamaš, and it is probable that quite a few of them were named Ebabbar.[17] But the temple of Šamaš at Mari was called Egirzalanki, not Ebabbar.[18]

If Erišti-Aya resided in a cloister in a city other than her own, of those known to us the most logical choice would be Sippar. Sippar had a famous cloister which evidently attracted women from many different locales. It also had a famous temple dedicated to Šamaš named Ebabbar.[19] The most serious drawbacks to such an identification are the slightly variant greeting invocations used by Erišti-Aya, the fact that contacts between Mari and Sippar are but rarely attested,[20] and most especially, the lack of evidence that a princess from one kingdom would serve as a priestess in another kingdom.

In spite of these last mentioned difficulties, the supposition that Erišti-Aya was writing from the cloister in Sippar is virtually certain. An unpublished text supplies us with the missing connection. The text is reported to say (in part): "To Zimri-Lim say this: Thus (says) the prophet of Šamaš. This is what Šamaš, the lord of the country, says: 'Let them send quickly to me to Sippar for (your own) life the throne destined for my residence of splendor--as well as your daughter which I have (already) requested of you.'"[21] The daughter requested by Šamaš, to be one of his *nadiātum* no doubt, is surely none other than Erišti-Aya![22]

Because Erišti-Aya was a princess, her situation may not have been exactly typical of other *nadiātum*. Nevertheless, she may not have been exactly atypical either, for as Harris has pointed out, most *nadiātum* "came from highly regarded families, from the class of officialdom."[23] We may suspect that the *nadītum*, whose servant is mentioned in IX 24.iii. 16, if indeed she is not identical with Erišti-Aya, was also of high or even royal rank, since her servant is supported out of the palace storeroom. Because of the cryptic nature of V 82, we can say nothing about the status of the *nadītum* mentioned in that text, escept that she probably was not of high station.[24]

From Erišti-Aya's letters, one fact emerges very clearly: the principal function of the *nadītum*, at least in this case, was a religious one.[25] She performed a vital service for the king in praying continually for him and for his dynasty (*bīt abika*) before Šamaš and Aya, especially the latter. Erišti-Aya frequently had to remind her father of this fact; although she faithfully performed her duties, she was not receiving her due rations from the royal stores. On occasion, she may simply state that she is praying for her father: *a-na ka-ka-bi-ia a-bi-ia qí-bí-ma um-ma e-ri-iš-ti-*ᵈ*a-a-ma ka-ri-ib-ta-ka* "To my Star, my father, say thus (says) Eristi-Aya, the one who prays for you" (X 42.1-4). Sometimes the affirmation of her intercessory role is linked with her lack of provisions: [*ù*(?) DU]MU.MÍ É-*k*[*a* ...] ŠE.BA SÍG.BA *ù* KAŠ.DÙG[.GA] *i-ma-ḫa-ra a-na-ku iš-ti-a-at-ma ka-ri-ib-ta-ka ú-ul pa-aq-da-ku a-na ba-l*[*a-ṭ*]*í-ka ša-am-ša-am ù ši-we-ri ak-ru-ub-ma ši-we-ri ù ša-*[*am-ša-am*] ᵐ*er-mi-*ᵈIM [ ] *am-ti-šu* [ ] "Now the daughter(s) of your house...are receiving their rations of grain, clothing, and good beer. But even though I alone am the woman who prays for you, I am not provisioned! I dedicated a sun(-disk) and my ring(-money)[26] for your life but then Ermi-Addu [took] my ring(-money) and the sun (-disk) [for] his servant" (X 40.1´-10´). Similarly, another letter, although badly broken, seems to contain an admonition to send supplies, so that she may be able to pray for the king (?) during the festival:[27] *i-na i-sí-nim*[...] *lu-uk-ru-b*[*a-ak-ku-um*] (X 42.11´-12´). But most commonly, Erišti-Aya points to her role as the sacred emblem (*šurinnum*) of Zimri-Lim when complaining about her lack of provisions: [*a-na-ku ú-u*]*l šu-ri-nu-um ka-ri-bu-um ša* É A.BA *a-na mi-nim la pa-aq-da-a-ku* "Am I not the praying emblem of (your) father's house? Why am I not provisioned?" (X 36.13-18); *šu-ri-in* É *a-bi-ka a-na-ku a-na mi-nim la pa-aq-da-a-ku* KÙ.BABBAR *ù* Ì.GIŠ *ú-ul i-di-nu-nim* "I am the emblem of your father's house. Why am I not provisioned? They have not given me money or oil!" (X 39.20-24); [*a-n*]*a-ku ú-ul šu-ri-nu-um* [*k*]*a-ri-bu-um* [*ša*] *a-na ba-la-ṭí-ka* [*ik*]*-ta-na-ra-bu* [*a-n*]*a mi-nim it-ti a-bi-ia* [Ì.G]IŠ LÀL! *la pa-aq-da-ku* "Am I not your praying emblem who constantly prays for your life? Why am I not provisioned with oil and honey from my father?" (X 37.7-12);

a-na-ku ú-ul šu-ri-in-ka-a ka-ri-bu-um ša i-na é-(babbar)babbar-ri-im i-gi-ri-ka ú-da-ma-qú "Am I not your praying emblem who gives you a good reputation in Ebabbar?" (X 38.9-11).

The use of the word *šurinnum* "(sacred) emblem" in these texts seems to be unique.[28] The basic concept of *šurinnum* seems to be that of an emblem or standard of a deity, a visible object which represents the deity in a certain locale. Often the *šurinnum* itself assumed divine qualities, undoubtedly because of its close association with the deity it represented. *Šurinnum* may also mean simply "emblem, standard." In this last sense, *šurinnum* may be used as the emblem of a city, a region, a guild, or an individual;[29] less clear is the meaning of *šurinnum* (Sumerian: š u - n i r) when applied to ships or wagons or doors.[30] Nevertheless, in no other case known to me is the *šurinnum* itself said to be a human being. Yet in these letters from Mari, Erišti-Aya emphatically says that she herself is the *šurinnum*. Thus, in an original but apt metaphor, Erišti-Aya underscores her importance to the king and his welfare as his personal representative before the gods Šamaš and Aya, praying for his welfare and that of his house.

Erišti-Aya's metaphor of herself as the *šurinnum* of the king, who prays continually for his life, should be compared to the common practice of installing votive statues before the god(s) in the temple. These votive statues were thought to offer effectively continuous prayer on behalf of the donor. They could be of two types. The first was a representation of the donor himself in some gesture of prayer.[31] The second type was a depiction of protective genii (*lamassātum*), or the like, who prayed on the donor's behalf.[32] This second type is the one comparable to the role of Erišti-Aya. Both types were installed by the king as intercessors to pray continuously for him in his absence.

Other *nadiātum* of Sippar also act as intercessors on behalf of their fathers. While they do not employ Erišti-Aya's *šurinnum*-metaphor, they do term themselves as "the one who prays continually for you/your life." Thus a *nadītum* writing to her father, from whom she is seeking a favor, reminds him none too subtly that "I continually pray for you with washed hands before my lord and my lady."[33] Another *nadītum*, concerned over the poor health of her father, wrote him two almost identical letters reminding him that she was praying for his health: "(During my) morning and evening offerings before my lord and my lady, I pray continually for your life."[34] Although other persons, especially women, performed similar acts of piety,[35] praying for their fathers and benefactors seems to have been considered part of the regular role of the *nadiātum*.[36] In the case of Erišti-Aya it may have been the primary motive of her *nadītum*-ship; at least it is the role Erišti-Aya stresses when she complains.

The gods before whom Erišti-Aya prayed were Šamaš and his consort Aya, the gods to whom the *nadiātum* of Sippar were dedicated. Harris has pointed out that the *nadiātum* had a closer attachment and a more personal relationship with Aya than with Šamaš. This situation seems to be borne out in the letters of Erišti-Aya as well. Twice Erišti-Aya makes mention of her activities specifically toward Aya. In the first she remarks that she has brought the garment and jar (of ointment, no doubt), which Zimri-Lim had sent to her *a-na be-el-ti-ia mu-ba-lí-ṭì-ka* "to my lady (Aya), who preserves your (Zimri-Lim) life" (X 38.24-25). In the second instance Erišti-Aya requests the king to "send me oil. I have to go and anoint the body of my lady (Aya)" (Ì.GIŠ *šu-bi-lam pa!-ga-ar be-el-ti-ia a-pa-⌈ša⌉-aš-ši*, X 41.5´-7´).[38] There are no comparable references to Šamaš. He is mentioned only in the introductory formulae cited above containing references to both Šamaš and Aya (*bēlī u bēltī*). Samas is also implicitly included in the *nadītum*'s remark that she is constantly interceding for her father in Ebabbar (X 38.9-11). This text provides the evidence necessary for showing the close ties that the *nadiātum* had with the Šamaš temple, evidence which Harris found strangely lacking in the Sippar materials.[39]

As was normal in these matters, the decision to have Erišti-Aya enter the cloister was her parents'. In a letter to the queen, her mother, Erišti-Aya states, *mu-ut-ki ù at-ta*(sic!) *a-na ga-gi-*[*i*]*m tu-še*$_{20}$*-ri-ba-ni-*[*i*]*n-*⌈*ni*⌉ "your husband and you made me enter the cloister" (X 43.15-17). Erišti-Aya implies that she was not completely in accord with her parents' decision. How her parents came to this decision is unclear. However, this statement by Erišti-Aya would seem to indicate that the "request" of Šamaš[40] came only after the decision had been taken by Zimri-Lim. Šamaš' request was thus perhaps an affirmative reply by the temple personnel to an inquiry from the Mari monarch about the suitability of donating a throne to Šamaš and at the same time devoting his daughter to the service of the god as a *nadītum*. Apart from the obvious religious advantage of having a personal representative before Šamaš,

Zimri-Lim may have been influenced by the prestige of having a daughter among the Sippar *nadiātum*, as did his contemporaries on the throne in Babylon.[41]

Since much of Erišti-Aya's correspondence concerns the matter of her support, a word must be said about her dowry. Although the term dowry (*šeriktum*) is not used in these letters, Erišti-Aya was provided, it seems, with a dowry upon entering the cloister. In an impassioned letter to her mother, complaining of neglect, she states:

> DUMU.MÍ LU[GAL *a-na-ku*]
> *aš-ša-a*[*t* LUGAL]
> *at-ti e-zu-ub tup-p*[*a-tim*]
> *ša mu-ut-ki ù at-ta*(sic!)
> *a-na ga-gi-*[*i*]*m*
> *tu-še*$_{20}$*-ri-ba-ni-*[*i*]*n-*⌈*ni*⌉
> *re-du-ú ša i-na ša-la-tim*
> *i-le-qú-ú-nim*
> *ú-da-ma-qú*
> *ù at-ti ia-ti*
> *du-mi-qí-ni*
>
> I am a king's daughter! You are a king's wife! Even disregarding the tablets with which your husband and you made me enter the cloister--they treat well soldiers taken as booty! You, then, treat me well! (X 43.12-22).

With due caution, I speculate that the "tablets" referred to contained the terms of her dowry, as stipulated in the Code of Hammurapi: *šum-ma* NIN.DINGIR LUKUR *ù lu sé-ek-ru-um ša a-bu-ša še-ri-ik-tam iš-ru-ku-ši-im tup-pa-am iš-ṭú-ru-ši-im i-na tup-pí-im ša iš-ṭú-ru-ši-im* "In the case of an *entum*, a *nadītum*, or a *sekrum*, whose father, upon presenting a dowry to her, wrote a tablet for her, if he did not write for her on the tablet which he wrote for her," etc.[42] Whether Erišti-Aya had absolute control over her dowry is unclear. At least she was dependent upon the royal officials back in Mari for shipment of provisions to her in Sippar. These provisions were often slow in coming, occasioning the letters in which she stressed the extreme straits to which she had been reduced: *ip-ri lu-bu-ši ša* A.BA *ú-*<*ba-*>*la-ṭa-an-ni*[43] *i-di-nu-nim-ma li-*

di-nu-nim la ba-ri-a-ku "My rations of grain and clothing, with which (my) father keeps me alive, they (once) gave me, so let them give me (them now) lest I starve (X 36.22-26).[44]

The provisions that Erišti-Aya expected involved the usual rations: grain and clothing (*ip-ra-am lu-bu-ša-am*, X 36.19; cf. 22), clothing, honey, and choice oil (*lu-bu-ši* LAL *ù* Ì.GIŠ, X 37.24-25), (slave-girls) and clothing (*lu-bu-ši*, X 38.20), money[45] and oil (KÙ.BABBAR *ù* Ì.GIŠ, X 39.23), oil (Ì.GIŠ, X 41.5´), grain, clothing, and good beer (ŠE.BA SÍG.BA *ù* KAŠ. DÙG[.GA], X 40.2´). Although most of the provisions Erišti-Aya requested were for her own maintenance, certain items were, on occasion, used for cultic purposes.[46]

Erišti-Aya's protestations of poverty are no doubt exaggerations, a stylistic feature common in Old Babylonian letters. Nevertheless there does seem to have been a certain estrangement between her royal parents and herself. For even in areas where she could reasonably have expected her actions to be well received at court, she seems to have suffered rebuff. In her letter to her mother she protests that she has been insulted: *a-na mi-nim ṣú-ba-ti la ta-al-ta-ab-ši-i-ma tu-te-ri-im-ma pí-iš-tam ù er-re-e-tam te-me-di-*[*in-ni*] "Why have you not put on my garment (which I sent you)? (Instead) you have returned[47] (it) to me and (so) inflicted slander and curses upon me!" (X 43.7-11).[48] She seems to have been similarly rebuffed by her father:[49] *ṣú-ba-tam ša ki-ma* [*lu*?*-b*]*u-uš-ti-ka a-qí-iš-ma šu-mi ú-ul iz-ku-ur* "I presented (to you) a garment like your (own) clothing,[50] but he paid no attention to me"[51] (X 39.29-31). Even if Erišti-Aya is imagining things or exaggerating, she evidently felt a certain estrangement from the royal court, which could only have been reinforced by the distance which separated Mari and Sippar.

In Sippar "probably every *nadītum* owned at least one slave and many had several. These slaves took care of the many menial tasks required in the household."[52] Just how many slaves Erišti-Aya owned is not known, but a large segment of her correspondence deals with this subject. In one letter there is mention of both a male and a female slave, but the broken state of the text precludes more explicit detail (X 36.8-9). Elsewhere only female slaves are involved. The slaves were supplied to her by her father: 2 GEMÉ *ša-da-aq-di-im tu-ša-bi-lam-ma* 1 GEMÉ *im-tu-ut-ti i-na-an-na* 2 GEMÉ *ub-lu-nim* 1 GEMÉ *im-tu-ut-ti-ma* "Last year you sent me two female slaves and one (of those) slaves had to go and die! Now they have brought me two (more) female slaves (and of these) one slave had to go and die! (X 39.15-19).[53]

In the letter to her mother Erišti-Aya requests another governess, more to her liking:

> *ù ta-ri-tam a-ṭà-ra-a-di ša ḫa-di-ia*
> *šu-bi-lam-ma lu-uḫ-du a-aḫ-ka*(sic!)
> *e-li-ia la ta-na-di-i*
>
> Now I simply must send back[54] the governess! Send me (another) of my liking that I may be happy. Do not be lax as regards me (X 43.27-29).

The presence here of a governess is curious.[55] Does this imply that Erišti-Aya entered the cloister as a mere youth? One should recall here the hypothesis that *nadiātum* were dedicated to the god from birth.[56]

Still more perplexing are the female slaves which Erišti-Aya refers to as GEMÉ *limdātiya* (X 38.12-13, 19). The dictionaries list no vocable **limdatu* or **limittu*.[57] Hence we are limited to internal evidence for the meaning of this phrase. Further information on the nature of these slaves is contained in a passage from another letter, unfortunately incomplete. The latter passage reads: [(x)]x-*ma ša*? [...] *la-am-da-a-ku* 2 GEMÉ *tu-la-mi-da-ni a-na mi-nim a-na* 1 GEMÉ *tu*!*-te-er* GEMÉ? *šu-bi-lam* "...in which(?)...I am skilled(?),[58] you have trained two female slaves for me. Why have you reneged(?) on one slave? Send me the (other) slave(?)!" (X 42.1′-6′). Evidently the king was supposed to train two of Erišti-Aya's slaves, in what art we are not informed, and then send them back to his daughter. Why he subsequently returned only one is also not stated. At any rate, it appears that GEMÉ *limdātiya* must mean "the slaves trained for me," i.e., an objective genitive. The whole passage may thus be translated: *a-na mi-nim* 2 SAG.GEMÉ *li*!*-im-da-ti-ia* [*t*]*a-ap-ru-ús* [ ]x *šu* x[xx] *ri* ⌜*tu*⌝*-ša-bi-lam* 1 GEMÉ *ta-ap-ta-ra-às i-na-an-na a-nu-um-ma* 2 GEMÉ *li-im-da-ti-ia ù lu-bu-ši šu-bi-lam* "Why have you singled out the two female slaves that were trained for me? ....you have sent me. One of the female slaves you have singled out! Now then send me (both of) the two female slaves that were trained for me--and (also send me) my ration of clothes!" (X 38.12-21). Again we are not told just what the slaves were to be trained in, but whatever it was, it was specifically for Erišti-Aya's purposes.[59]

From the texts preserved for us, we can see that Erišti-Aya had at a minimum three--and perhaps as many as seven--slaves at one time. And in all probability there were more. We may suppose, then, that even in the cloister her royal rank was fairly well maintained despite her disclaimers to the contrary.

Conclusion

Erišti-Aya has been shown to be a *nadītum* living in the great cloister complex at Sippar. The circumstances surrounding her entry into the cloister are not entirely clear, although a message from the prophet of Šamaš of Sippar claimed that the god had earlier requested this daughter of Zimri-Lim. There is some evidence that all *nadiātum* prayed for their fathers and/or benefactors. This is certainly the case with Erišti-Aya. Indeed, her principal role, as it emerges from these letters, is that of *kāribtum*, praying continually for the life/welfare of her royal father. This intercessory role even seems to have been alluded to in the oracle in which Zimri-Lim was requested to send his daughter, for no doubt the publication of the text will show that not only the throne but also "the daughter which I have requested of you" were to be sent "for (your own) life."[60]

In general, Erišti-Aya's letters portray her in a manner that accords well with the portrait of the *nadītum* as sketched by Rivkah Harris. Certain details emerge more clearly, for example, the close connection with the Šamaš temple. Other differences may be attributed to Erišti-Aya's status as a princess and a foreigner.[61]

NOTES TO CHAPTER 5

ERIŠTI-AYA, A *NADĪTUM*

[1]This chapter is to a large extent dependent upon previous studies on the *nadītum*, especially those of Rivkah Harris: "*Nadītu*," 106-35; "Cloister," 121-57; "Biographical Notes on the *Nadītu* Women of Sippar," *JCS* 16 (1962), 1-12; and J. Renger, *Priestertum* I, 149-76.

[2]Definite occurrences of the word *nadītum* are V 82. 19 and IX 24.iii.16. There is possibly another occurrence in X 37.15 ([...]*na*?*di-tam*), but the fragmentary character of this text precludes certainty.

[3]See also *abiya* (X 37.11; 39.10) and A.BA (X 36.16, 23), both of which clearly refer to Zimri-Lim.

[4]See Moran, *Biblica* 50 (1969), 33.

[5]*bēltum* is the habitual title of the queen at Mari, see above, chap. 1, p. 9. Erišti-Aya was not the only princess to become a *nadītum*. Of the *nadiātum* who inhabited the cloister at Sippar, at least three were princesses. The earliest of them was Ayalatum, the daughter of Sumu-la-ila, the second ruler of the first dynasty of Babylon. Two other princesses bore the name Iltani. The earlier Iltani was the daughter of Sin-muballiṭ and was thus the sister of Ḫammurapi. The later Iltani seems to have been the daughter of either Samsuiluna or Abi-ešuḫ. On these princesses, see Harris, *JCS* 16 (1962), 6f.; "*Nadītu*," 123.

[6]*Ibid.*, pp. 126-28.

[7]*Ibid.*, pp. 117, 119.

[8]*mādiš ūmī*, while rare, is attested for the OB period elsewhere at Larsa (YOS 2 39:4-5), Uruk (*BagM* 2, 56, I, 6-7), and Ur (*UET* 5, 70, 4-6; 82, 4-6; 71, 4-6). See Erkki Salonen, *Die Gruss- und Höflichkeitsformeln in babylonisch-assyrischen Briefen* (Helsinki, 1967), 63.

[9]*Ibid.*, p. 53.

[10]A 3525:7, unpub. OB letter, quoted by *CAD* E 309b; cf. *ki-*[*m*]*a šamê*(AN) *ù ir-ṣe-*[*tim*] *a* x [*d*]*a-a lu d*[*a-r*]*i* "As the heaven and the earth..may he be everlasting" (PBS 7 59:7-8).

[11]On the cloister and the *nadītum*, see "Cloister," 121f.; Renger, *Priestertum* I, 146.

[12]For example, the *ugbabtum*; see Renger, *Priestertum* I, 146.

[13]"*Nadītu*," 132.

[14]*MSL* 12, 96, l. 96.

[15]See above, n. 5.

[16]For Awat-Aya, sister of Gimiliya of Babylon, and Eli-eressa, daughter of Naḫ-ila of Dilbat, who also lived in the cloister at Sippar, see Harris, *JCŠ* 16 (1962), 3-4 and n. 7; "*Nadītu*," 131-32. See further Harris, *JESHO* 13 (1970), 316, on CT 48, 18.

[17]In addition to Sippar, Larsa and Lagash are known to have had temples dedicated to Šamaš under the name of Ebabbar; see Ebeling, *RLA* II, 263. However, the Šamaš temple at Babylon was named Edikukalamma (é - d i -

k u$_5$ - k a l a m - m a); see *ibid.*, p. 475, s.v. Esakudkalamma; Renger, "Götternamen in der altbabylonischen Zeit," *Heidelberger Studien zum alten Orient* (Wiesbaden, 1967), 140.

[18]Written *e-gi-ir-za-la-an-ki* (= é - g i r$_x$(KA) - z a l - a n - k i.). See Dossin, *Syria* 32 (1955), 15, iv.11; the Akkadian equivalent is given as É *ta-ši-la-at ša-mi-e ù er-ṣi-tim* "Temple, the luxuriation of Heaven and Earth."

[19]Larsa and Lagash, while they also had temples with the name of Ebabbar, are eliminated from consideration because no *nadiātum* are known to have resided in Lagash, while those known from Larsa were all *nadiātum* of gods other than Šamaš and Aya; see Renger, *Priestertum* I, 170-73.

[20]II 24.15´; 122.5; VI 27.13´.

[21]"A Zimri-Lim dis ceci: ainsi (parle) le prophète (*âpilum*) de Šamaš. Voice ce qu'a dit Šamaš, le seigneur du pays: 'Qu'on m'envoie rapidement à Sippar pour la vie' ([*an*]*a balâṭim*) le trône destiné à ma résidence de splendeur, ainsi que ta fille que je t'ai (déjà) demandés" (A. 4260), G. Dossin, "Prophétisme," 85.

[22]This writer was pleased to note that his independent conclusion had been anticipated by K. R. Veenhof, *BiOr* 25 (1968), 198; and by Romer, *Frauenbriefe* 17, who also adduces text A. 4260; so also Sasson, "Royal Ladies," 77-78. On the other hand, the statement of Renger, *Priestertum* II, 219, n. 1048, "es handelt sich hier sicher um einen Tempel des Šamaš von Sippar in Mari," cannot be maintained.

One cannot but wonder about the significance of the name Erišti-Aya "Request of Aya" in this case and its relation to the text just cited, "your daughter which I have requested of you," a relationship which would be particularly striking should the verb employed in this case turn out to be a form of *erēšu*. If Šamaš had made his previous request in the recent past, that would lend support to Harris's ("*Nadītu*," 128) contention that the names of many *nadiātum* were assumed at the time they entered the cloister rather than to Renger's (*Priestertum* I, 153) opinion that these women were dedicated to the god from birth and given their names from childhood. But see below, p. 101.

[23]"*Nadītu*," 123.

[24]See Renger, *Priestertum* I, 169f.

[25]The economic factors which Harris ("*Nadītu*," 109) has shown to be of primary importance to the parent whose daughter has entered the cloister were inoperative in this case.

[26]Cf. *CAD* K 197, s.v. *karābu* 5a.

[27]The festival was no doubt the *isinnum ša Šamaš*. On this festival, which was held on the twentieth day of the month in Sippar, see "*Nadītu*," 115-16; Landsberger, *Kult. Kalender*, 137f. This festival is attested at Mari during the Assyrian interregnam (VII 13.8).

[28]For the latest treatment of *šurinnum*, see Sjöberg, "Zu einigen Verwandtschaftsbezeichnungen in Sumerischen," in *Heidelberger Studien zum alten Orient*, 205f, n. 9; and J. Krecher, "Göttersymbole und -attribute," *RLA*, III, 497.

[29]Sjöberg, *loc. cit.*

[30]For g i š - š u - n i r - m á "emblem of a ship," see A. Salonen, *Wasserfahrzeuge*, 79, n. 1, and 124f. For š u - n i r - g i g̃ i r (a) "emblem of a wagon," see A. Salonen, *Landfahrzeuge*, 131. For *šurinnu ša bābi* "emblem of a door," see A. Salonen, *Die Türen*, 93 and 146.

[31]Many examples from various sites have been conveniently gathered by Spycket, *Les statues de culte* (Paris, 1968); the materials from Mari for this period are cited on pp. 94-98.

[32]In Babylon the practice is well documented from OB year names; see, for example, Ammiditana year no. 29, for which the Akkadian translation reads: *ša-at-tum ša am-mi-di-ta-na šar-rum* ^{d}*la-ma-sà-at meš-re-e ša a-na ba-la-ṭi-šu i-kar-ra-bu i-na* KÙ.GI *ru-ši-im ù* NA_4 *a-qar-tim ib-ni-i-ma a-na* ^{d}INNANA NIN HUŠ.KI.A *mu-ul-li-a-at šar-ru-ti-šu ú-še-lu-ú* "The year in which Ammiditana the king dedicated to Ištar, the great lady---who gave him his kingship, the (status of the) protective genii of prosperity who pray for his life, which he constructed out of brilliant-red gold and precious stones"; see M. Schorr, VAB 5, 603; and A. Ungnad, *RLA* 2, 189. For other examples, see *ibid.*, 188f., Ammiditana #23, and 190, Ammiṣaduqa #7. See further von Soden, "Die Schutzgenien lamassu und schedu in der babylonisch-assyrischen Literatur," *BagM* 3 (1964), 148-56, esp. 154; A. L. Oppenheim, *Ancient Mesopotamia*, 198-206.

[33]*maḫar bēliya u bēltiya qatāya masiāma aktanarrabakku* (PBS 7 60 25-28).

[34]*kurummat*(ŠUK) *kaṣâtim u līliātim maḫar bēliya u bēltiya ana balāṭika aktanarrab* (PBS 7 105 13-15 = 106 8-10). See also PBS 7 125, which seems to have been written by a *nadītum* (note the *gagûm* in Sippar, l. 26), in which she styles herself *kāribtakī* "the one who prays for you" (ll. 10, 15, 28, 31).

[35]See below, chap. 10, pp. 129-31.

[36]K. R. Veenhof, *BiOr* 25 (1968), 197f., suggests that there is "some relation between the fact that many *nadiātum* (of Šamaš in Sippar and Ninurta in Nippur) have names of the type *Lamassī*, *Lamassāni*, *Lamassatum* and the fact that one of their functions or perhaps duties in the *gagûm* was to pray for their relatives, as evidenced by the self-designation *karibtaka*." This is evidently correct; our discussion of Erišti-Aya's use of the *šurinnum*-metaphor points in the same direction.

[37]"*Nadītu*," 116-22.

[38]Sasson has suggested to me the reading for line 6′-7′: *ši-pí ši-ri*(!) *be-el-ti-ia a-pa-*[*ša*]*-aš-ši* "so that I can anoint the feet and body of my lady," from which my own reading is partially derived. *a-pa-*⌈*ša*⌉*-aš-ši* is evidently the *i*-modal verb form; see below, n. 53.

[39]"Cloister," 155-56.

[40]See above, p. 95.

[41]See above, n. 5.

[42]CH #178, see also #179. These two sections envision the case of a father providing his daughter with a dowry, whether she has absolute title to it or not; #180-181, on the other hand, show that the matter of providing a dowry was optional. In the latter case, however, the father must have maintained his daughter out of his own income, since after the death of the father the daughter has the right to maintenance out of the paternal estate.

[43]I owe the reading of this line to Moran.

[44]This seems to have been a common complaint, however, among the *nadiātum* at Sippar (see *CAD* B, s.v. *barû* B 1a 2´): *ki-ma ba-ri-a-ku ú-ul aq-bi-ku-um* "Did I not tell you that I am starving? (And you said 'I will send you barley and sesame oil')" (TCL 1 26:6f.); *a-di-na-ni-ku-nu ba-ri-a-ku* 1 ŠE.GUR.TA.ÀM *šu-bi-la-nim-ma lu-uk-ru-ba-ku-nu-ši-im* "On your (MP) account I am starving! Send me one *gur* of barley so that I may pray for you" (*ibid.*, l. 18f.); *bi-re-ku ù ku-ṣú ik-ta-<aš>-du-ni-ni e-ri-ši-ia-ma* "I am hungry, and the cold has come upon me in my nakedness!" (TCL 1 23:19f., correction and translation courtesy of Moran); *i-na* A.ŠÀ-*ia* 3 ŠE.GUR *e-il-qí-e ba-ri-a-ku* "I took 3 *gur* of barley from my field, (for) I am starving!" (Fish, *Letters* 6:40-1); *am-mi-ni*[*m*] *ba-ri-a-*[*ku*] *di-a-ti-i la ta-ša-al i-na bi-ti-ka ma-an-nu-um bi-ri a-na-ku-ú ba-ri-a-ku-ú* "How can you not care when I go hungry? Who (else) is hungry in your house? Should (only) I go hungry?" (VAS 16 5:6f.); *i-na-an-na a-na-ku ba-ri-*[*a-ku*] *ù ma-ra-at-ki ba-ri-*[*a-at*] "Just now I am starving and your daughter is starving!" (VAS 16 102:8f.). These complaints may reflect a certain stylization, which detracts somewhat from our sense of immediacy. On the proneness of *nadiātum* to complain, see Harris, *JCS* 16 (1962), 7 with n. 20.

[45]Instead of "money" (KÙ.BABBAR), perhaps one should read "honey" (LÀL), after the parallel passage in X 37.25.

[46]See above, p. 98.

[47]Possibly *tuterrīm* has here the force of the G-stem and is used in hendiadys with the following verb, in which case the garment was not actually returned. Nevertheless, the sense is approximately the same.

[48]Compare the queen's request of her husband that he honor her by wearing the garments which she has made: *ù a-nu-um-ma* 1 TÚG ù GÚ.È.A *ša e-pu-šu be-lí a-na bu-di-šu li-iš-ku-un* "And, now let my lord place on his shoulder the garment and the cloak which I have made" (X 17.9-13).

[49]This letter is addressed to *šamšiya*. This title was also in X 99.5; compare the overly cautious statement of Römer, *Frauenbriefe*, 4.

[50]Instead of [*lu-b*]*u-uš-ti-ka*, perhaps read [*b*]*u-uš-ti-ka* "which is like (i.e. worthy of) your dignity."

[51]In ll. 30-31 on the edge of the tablet, there is present a division in the middle of the lines which was not clearly indicated by the scribe, so that in reality there are four lines, not two. On the expression *šumam zakārum*, see Kraus, *RA* 64 (1971), 99-112.

[52]"*Nadītu*," 134.

[53]For the *i*-modal verb form ("action under compulsion") involved in *imtutti*, see Jacobsen, *JNES* 22 (1963), 27f.; see also von Soden, *Ergänzungsheft zum GAG* #82 e. J. Sasson has kindly called my attention to this verbal form.

Presumably this case of 50 percent mortality in two years is exceptional, for even Erišti-Aya seems to think that this is a little too much! One cannot but wonder whether their deaths are to be attributed only to Erišti-Aya's unusual ill-fortune or whether their deaths tell us something about the quality of the slaves her parents sent her.

[54]Again the verb form is *i*-modal, with secondary lengthening; see preced-

ing note. The writer acknowledges Moran as the source of this interpretation.

[55]A *tāritum* is listed among those receiving rations from the palace stores in IX 24.iv.51.

[56]See above, n. 22.

[57]Cf. Römer, *Frauenbriefe*, 69, n. 4; Sasson, "Royal Ladies," 78 ("apprentice"). Moran has called my attention to the occurrences of this vocable in Tell Asmar 31-T 299:12.

[58]It seems that *lamdāku*, despite its G-stative form, may have the meaning of the D-stem, hence "I am trained," rather than the expected "that which...I have learned."

[59]From the ration lists of the palace archives we learn the name of Aya-arri, the female slave of an unnamed *nadītum*: 40 (SÌLA) ^d*a-ia-ar-ri* *ša na-di-tim* (IX 24.iii.16). It is entirely possible that Aya-arri is the name of one of the female slaves of Erišti-Aya mentioned above. No other *nadītum* in the time of Zimri-Lim is known to us from Mari. And the fact that the slave is supported out of the palace storehouse makes it probable that she is one of the very slaves that Erišti-Aya requests be sent to her.

[60]See above, n. 21.

[61]As a postscript, it is perhaps worth noting that Erišti-Aya is not the only daughter whom Zimri-Lim dedicated to religious service. He gave another daughter into the service of Adad of Appan. Unfortunately, our knowledge of this incident is limited to the cryptic information contained in two year names from the reign of this ruler; see year names nos. 23 and 24. Dossin, *SM*, 58.

CHAPTER 6

THE *ŠUGĪTUM*

Little can be said of the *šugītum* at Mari.[1] The word *šugītum* is only once certainly attested in the Mari documents, and this is unfortunately in a broken context. In a letter to Šibtu, Zimri-Lim writes:

aš-šum SAL.TUR DUMU.MÍ ^{m}*i-ba-*⸢*al*⸣-^{d}IM
šu-gi-tim ša ta-a[*š-pu-ri-im*]
an-ni-ki-a-am a-wa-tum [*im-qu-ut-ma*]
⸢*um-ma*⸣*-a-mi* SAL.T[UR]
[x x]*la*? *an n*[*i*?]
[*i-n*]*a-an-na ša* [SAL.TUR (*ša-ti*)]
wa-ar-ka-[ ]
pu-ur-ri[*-si*]
šum-ma SAL.TUR *ši-i* [*i-ša-ri-iš*]
nu-uz-zu-ma-at [ ]
i-na É [ ]
li-ši-ib ù šu[*m-ma i-ša-ri-iš*]
ú-ul nu-uz-zu-m[*a-at i-na* É ...]
li-ši-ib ù li-iṣ-ṣú-ru-[*ši*]

Concerning the young[2] daughter of Ibal-Addu, the *šugītum*, about whom you wrote me, word has reached here as follows: "The young woman...." Now then, about the matter of that young woman, investigate the case....[3] If that young woman is justly complained about, let her reside in the house of...; but if she is unjustly complained about, let her reside in the house of...and let them keep her under surveillance (X 124.4-17).

This letter is obviously connected with another letter in which the same persons are involved:

> [*ù?*] DUMU.MÍ *i-ba-al-*^{d}IM *i-ba*$^{?}$[*-aš*$^{?}$*-ši*$^{?}$]
> *aš-ra-nu-um-ma ki-li-e*[*-ši*]
> *la ta-ṭà-ra-di-iš-ši*
>
> And(?) the daughter of Ibal-Addu is present(?), detain her there; do not send her (X 123.27-29).

The instructions not to send the daughter of Ibal-Addu back to Zimri-Lim contrast with the instructions given in this same letter concerning the *ugbabātum* of Adad of Kulmiš or the female weavers who were captured as war slaves.[4] The possibility must be entertained that this daughter of Ibal-Addu was also a war slave. In the latter part of Zimri-Lim's reign, Ibal-Addu, the king of Ašlakka, was a vassal and ally of Zimri-Lim. However Aslakka was not always subservient to the king of Mari, for one of the regnal years of Zimri-Lim is named after his defeat of the town of Ašlakka.[5] A long fourteen column tablet probably contains the names of the numerous war slaves taken captive at this time.[6] Although Ibal-Addu was allowed to retain his throne, it seems that Ibal-Addu's daughter was taken to Mari as a hostage to insure her father's loyalty to the king of Mari. If this were indeed the case, it would explain why Zimri-Lim gave explicit orders that this woman was to be kept in Mari and under surveillance!

The exact nature of the complaint against this woman is now lost in the break. Did it have anything to do with her *šugītum*-ship? Likewise lost are the two alternatives as to where this *šugītum* was to reside. Nevertheless, since Ibal-Addu's daughter is singled out for a treatment different from that of the *ugbabātum*, who were explicitly spared the indignities of the textile factory, one wonders whether this woman may not have been assigned to the textile factory along with other women captured at this time.[7] If so, perhaps X 124.16f. is to be restored [*i-na* É ^{f}UŠ.BAR.MEŠ] *li-ši-ib* "let her reside in the house of the female-weavers."[8] The second alternative was apparently less demeaning; but in no case was she to be given complete freedom. Given all the uncertainties, however, no firm conclusions can be drawn.

The *šugītum* is not otherwise attested in these Mari texts. Hence little is added to our knowledge about the role or function of the *šugītum*.

NOTES TO CHAPTER 6

THE *ŠUGĪTUM*

[1]For the latest treatment of the *sugītum*, see Renger, *Priestertum* I, 176-79.

[2]This translation is based upon a comparison of texts such as I 77.8; III 8.6; X 140.16; 114.5, etc., where SAL.TUR functions as a descriptive qualification of the following word. Also possible is the construct: "the slave-girl of the daughter of Ibal-Addu, the *šugītum*," in which case the *šugitum* may be either the slave-girl or Ibal'Addu's daughter.

[3]See *AHw*, 832, where this passage is cited: *warka*[ ] *pu-ur-ri-*[*si*(?)].

[4]See above, chap. 4, pp. 81ff., for this incident.

[5]*šanat Zimrī-Lim Ašlakkā*[ki] *iṣbatu* "the year in which Zimri-Lim captured Ašlakka," year no. 2, and cf. year no. 3, *SM*, 54.

[6]XIII 1. On the relation of this tablet to the capture of Ašlakka, see the remarks of Dossin, *Syria* 41 (1964), 21-24.

[7]See above, n. 4.

[8]Cf. X 126, esp. l. 7; see above, chap. 4, p. 83.

CHAPTER 7

THE *QADIŠTUM*

The *qadištum* is attested but once in the Mari documents.[1] From this brief mention of the priestess little can be discerned, other than her identity: [f]*qa-di-iš-tum* / *ša an*ʹ-[*nu-*]*ni-*⌜*tim*⌝ [f]DUMU -*si-im-a-al* "The *qadištum* of Annunitum(?), a woman of the Sim'alite tribe..." (X 59.3ʹ-4ʹ). Despite the cryptic character of this text, several deducations may be made. First, that this *qadištum* is not identified by name but only as the *qadištum* of Annunitum indicates that there was only one such priestess in the service of this goddess.[2] That no other *qadištum* is so far attested in the Mari materials is evidence that there were probably relatively few of these priestesses in the Mari region.[3] This particular *qadištum* is said to be of the Sim'alite (or "northern") tribe. Despite the nomadic character of her ethnic origins, this particular woman appears to have resided in Mari, where she probably served in the temple of Annunitum.[5]

The publication of this Mari text undermines, in the mind of this writer, the attempts to see *qaššatum* as a dialectical variant of *qadištum*.[6] Just who those women were who in one of the tablets from Mari are identified as *qa-aš-ša-tum*[7] still remains enigmatic. But it now appears difficult to equate them with the *qadištum*. To postulate the existence of an otherwise unattested dialectical variant in simultaneous usage in one and the same locale with the universal and normal *qadištum* is most unlikely. The philological difficulties would seem to be borne out by the text itself, from which it is in no way apparent how these women can be considered priestesses. Granted that the purpose of the text is obscure,[8] it must be assumed that the *qaššatum*, for the purpose of this document, had a common status with the other women designated either as "slave (GEMÉ) of PN" or as "widow" (*almattum*). This writer sees no obvious common basis between these two last-named categories of women and the *qadištum*. Even if *qaššatum* should ultimately derive from the root *qdš*, it is not now apparent that *qaššatum* can be simply equated with *qadištum*. Consequently, the identity of the *qaššatum* must remain in doubt until further evidence is forthcoming.

NOTES TO CHAPTER 7

THE *QADIŠTUM*

[1]For the latest treatment of the *qadištum*, see Renger, *Priestertum* I, 179-84. The remarks of Astour, "Tamar the Hierodule: An Essay in the Method of Vestigial Motifs," *JBL* 85 (1966), 185-96, about the *qadištum* are not always reliable.

[2]In OB nonliterary texts, only two other examples of a *qadištum* in the service of a particular god are known; Renger, *Priestertum* I, 179.

[3]On the relatively small number of these priestesses, see *ibid.*, 182.

[4]On the DUMU(.MEŠ) *sim'āl*, see Kupper, *Les Nomades en Mésopotamie au temps des rois de Mari* (Paris, 1957), 54f. and 68.

[5]On this *qadištum*'s relationship to Addu-duri, see above, chap. 3, n. 30.

[6]This identification was first attempted by Birot, following a suggestion by Dossin, *Syria* 35 (1958), 20. The proposal, when presented at the *VI Rencontre Assyriologique Internationale*, was endorsed by Goetze but opposed by von Soden; see *BiOr* 13 (1956), 178a. Hirsch, *ZA* N.F. 22 (1964), 284, attempted to support the proposal by comparing Old Assyrian *kaššum* = *qaššum* < **qadšum* "holy." This identification was accepted by Renger, *Priestertum* I, 179, and later by von Soden, *AHw* 891 *qadištum*.

[7]IX 291.i.5 *et passim* in this text, = *Syria* 35 (1958), 9f. A variant *qa-aš-ša-at* occurs in i.21 and iv.20.

[8]Birot speculates that this text "peut avoir eu pour object de dresser une liste, dans la province de Terqa, des femmes susceptibles d'être facilement réquisitionnées," (*ARMT* IX, 344; see also *Syria* 35 [1958], 9-26). This writer, however, knows of no evidence which would support the contention that widows, personal slaves, or *qadištum* priestesses were traditionally subject to being requisitioned.

CHAPTER 8

THE *KEZERTUM*

This section on the *kezertum* is included in this study of priestesses with some hesitation. Although Assyriologists have generally assumed, on the basis of a single text, that the *kezertum* was some sort of priestess,[1] a few scholars have recently resisted making this identification.[2] However, since Renger[3] has again included the *kezertum* among the priestly class in his study of OB priesthood, it is necessary to include here a discussion of the Mari evidence for this identification.

The evidence for including the *kezrētum* among the ranks of the OB priesthood[4] is limited to a single letter in which Ḫammurapi gives instructions that certain (statues of) goddesses (*ištarātum*)[5] of Emutbalum are to be put on barges and brought to Babylon, along with certain *kezrētum*-women.[6] It has been universally assumed that these *kezrētum*-women were to accompany these divine images in the capacity of attendant priestesses. Admittedly this assumption is very attractive. Nevertheless, certain reservations must be maintained in view of the evidence regarding the function of *kezrētum* elsewhere.

Outside of Mari, the above-mentioned text is, to my knowledge, the only one dating to the OB period which mentions these women. The rest of the texts come from a much later (Neo-Babylonian) period and therefore must be used with caution in defining the function of the *kezertum* in the OB period. These late texts are unanimous in understanding the *kezretum*/*kazratum* as a kind of prostitute.[7] I do not wish to enter into a discussion of the religious nature of prostitution, except to note that its religious character alone does not qualify prostitutes to be included within the ranks of the clergy. But it might qualify them as part of the entourage of the (statues of) goddesses.

To return to the Mari evidence of the OB period, it is clear that it does not support the assumption that the *kezertum* was a preistess. Of the two texts known previously, one (VII 275.3) is so broken as to be virtually useless in this discussion. The second text (VII 206.6) is also broken, but enough is preserved to show that here the *[k]izrētum* are mentioned together with the women of the harem (*sekrētum*), the cleaning-ladies-of-the-outer-court (*kisalluḫātum*), and the female-scribe(s) and young female-singer(s). The impression gained from this text is that the *kezrētum* are one of several groups of female servants employed by the palace in one function or another.

There is now a third text which can be brought into the discussion. This is a letter from Zimri-Lim to a certain [Mal]ik-Ak[ka] (X 140):[8]

aš-šum SAL.TUR *ki!-zi-ir-tim*
[n]a-we-er-tim a-na ṣe-ri-[ki]
[šu]-ri-im ù i-na ri-ši-ki
[ú]-zu-uz-zi-im ša ta-aš-pu-⌜ri-im⌝
i-nu-ma ia-ás-ma-aḫ-^{d}IM *i-na ma-ri*^{ki}
ú-ṣú-ú É.GAL-*lum im-ma-ši-i[ʾ]*
ù iš-tu ša a-na ḫa-ar-ra-na-tim
at-ta-al-la-ku ša-al-la-tam ma-li
ša qa-ti-{ia} ik-šu-du
a-na mi-ṭì be-el te-re-tim [ú-m]a-al-li
[i]-na-an-na i-nu-ma a-na KASAL *[al-la-ku]*
i-na ša-al-la-tim ša qa-ti i-ka-aš-ša-du
^{f}*k[i-zi-]⌜ir⌝-tim ša i-na re-ši-ki*
iz-za-az-z[u] ú-ša-ar-ra-ak-ki-im

Concerning (my) sending to you a splendid young *kezertum* to be in your retinue, about which you wrote me. When Yasmaḫ-Addu left Mari, the palace was despoiled. And from the time I have been on one campaign after another, whatever war captives I took I handed over for the needs (lit., insufficiency)[9] of my administrators. Now then, when I go on (my next) campaign, I will send you a *k[ez]ertum* to be in your retinue from among the war captives which I take (X 140.16-29).

The *kezertum* requested by Malik-Akka is to be a personal servant in her service. It thus appears impossible that the *kezertum* would be a priestess --unless Malik-Akka were herself a priestess of a high rank, a possibility for which there is no evidence. Furthermore, it is implied that the palace in Mari would normally have had *kezrētum* included among its personnel. The previous *kezrētum* had been carried off by Yasmaḫ-Addu as he fled Mari before the invading army which brought Zimri-Lim to power,[10] thus making it necessary to replace them. Even the method by which the *kezertum* was to be acquired, namely, as a prisoner of war, favors the interpretation that she was but one of the many palace slaves similarly captured in war. Such practices were common in the ancient Near East.[11]

In summary, the evidence is insufficient for defining the function of the *kezertum* in the OB period. On the one hand, it would appear that in Babylon she may have been a priestess in that she appears to be an attendant in the service of goddesses. On the other hand, at Mari she seems to be merely some kind of servant. One wonders if perhaps her function were not the same in both instances. Perhaps the *kezrētum* of the Ḫammurapi letter performed the same type of menial service function for the goddess as the Mari evidence suggests they performed at Mari. Consequently, there may be no evidence at all for postulating that the *kezertum* was a priestess.

NOTES TO CHAPTER 8

THE *KEZERTUM*

[1]Ungnad, *Babylonische Briefe aus der Zeit der Hammurapidynastie* (= VAB 6), 313: "Hierodule" (see also the translation on p. 5); Waterman, *Royal Correspondence of the Assyrian Empire IV*, 221: "temple women" (also III, 336: "corresponding to *kizritu*, 'devotees' of Ishtar..."); Bezold, *Babylonisch-assyrisches Glossar* (Heidelberg, 1926), 139: "Freudenmädchen; Hierodule."

[2]Kraus, *Or* NS 16 (1947), 182, n. 2; von Soden, *AHw* 468: "eine Dirne mit *kizirtu*-Haartracht"; *CAD* K 314f.: "prostitute (lit., woman with curled hair, a hair-do characteristic of a special status)."

[3]Renger, *Priestertum* I, 188.

[4]Perhaps one should also include here the Sumerian text which refers to *šugītum* priestesses wearing their hair like a *kezertum*, k i - s i k i l š u - g i_4 - a s a g - k i - g (ú) - l á - e (*SRT* I II 36 and dupl.); see Renger, *Priestertum* I, 179, n. 479. However, this text does not point so much to priesthood as to the hair-style worn by these priestesses.

[5]*CAD* I 270f. (similarly *CAD* K 315 s.v. *kezertum* A a) would have *ištarātum* here refer to the priestesses of that name. However, that is patently incorrect, as is evident from a comparison with VAB 6 3:4 *ilātim ša Emutbalim ṣābum ušallamakkum* "the men will bring the goddesses of Emutbalum safely to you," referring to the same event. This is also the manner in which all other translators have understood the text; see above, n. 1, and Renger, *Priestertum* I, n. 534; *AHw* 399 s.v. *ištaru(m)*; Spycket, *Les statues de culte*, 84.

[6]*AbB* 2, 34.

[7]In lexical series: *ša-am-ka-tum, ša-mu-uk-tum, ḫa-ar-ma-tum, ḫa-ri-im-tum, ka-az-ra-tum, ki-iz-re-tum* = KAR.KID (*CT* 18 19, K. 107+ i 31-36); in literature: *uptaḫḫir Ištar kezrēti šamḫāti u* SAL.KAR.KID.MEŠ "Ištar assembled the *kezrētum*, the pleasure-women and the prostitutes" (Gilgameš VI 165-66); *Uruk...āl kezrēti šamḫātu u ḫarimāt[i] ša Ištar mutu iṭerušinātima imnû qātušš[ūn]* "Uruk...the city of the *kezrētum*, the pleasure-women and the prostitutes, whom Ištar deprived of a husband/husbands and delivered into their hands" (*Era* IV 52-53; on this difficult passage, see Cagni, *L'Epopea di Erra*, 232); *kazratu pitquttu muttappilat šarrapti* "The discreet street prostitute slanders the...woman" (*BWL* 218:6).

[8]Dossin, "Documents de Mari," *Syria* 48 (1971), 5, treats this portion of X 140. My transliteration and translation, included here for convenience, differs only in details. See also Römer, *Freuenbriefe*, 55f.

Malik-Akka is otherwise unknown to me. Dossin must have restored this PN on the basis of unpublished material. Her identity is also problematic. Her interest in establishing diplomatic relations between Zimri-Lim and Adalšenni, king of Burundum (ll. 4-5), suggests that she was a highly placed woman, perhaps a queen, in one of the kingdoms in the vicinity of the latter king--but hardly his wife to judge from the tone of the letter. On Adalšenni, see Finet, "Adalšenni, roi de Burundum," *RA* 60 (1966), 17-28.

[9]Following Dossin, *Syria* 48 (1971), 5.

[10]The historical implications of this text should not be overlooked. We have little information as to the manner in which Zimri-Lim regained the throne of his father. From this text it appears that Yasmaḫ-Addu and the Assyrians withdrew from Mari alive and with enough ease that they were able to carry off the wealth of the city in the process. We are allowed to suppose that the Assyrians withdrew from Mari in the face of imminent attack by a superior force. This superior force was undoubtedly primarily the powerful army of Yarim-Lim, king of Aleppo and father-in-law of Zimri-Lim, a fact which may be deduced from the claims of Adad of Kallassu/Aleppo that he put Zimri-Lim upon his father's throne; see Lods, *Studies in Old Testament Prophecy Presented to T. H. Robinson*, ed. H. H. Rowley (Edinburgh, 1950), 103-4, and A. 2925, unpublished but quoted in translation by Dossin, "Sur le prophétisme à Mari," *Rencontre* XIV, 78f. See also Dossin, *BARB* 38 (1952), 235 published in translation only: "C'est mon père, en vérité, qui m'a fait remonter sur mon trône, c'est lui seul qui me soutiendra et qui affermira des fondements de mon trône..." For a (broken) text which mentions Zimri-Lim's(?) victory over Yasmaḫ-Addu at Tizraḫ, see Dossin, "Documents de Mari," *Syria*, 48 (1971), 2-6.

[11]A certain amount of caution, however, is warranted in the deduction that her acquisition by plundering bars the *kezertum* from being a priestess. Most war captives ended up as the slaves either of the palace or of a private citizen. When on occasion priestesses were taken captive--although such a practice was considered unethical--their dignity was carefully maintained; see above, chap. 4, pp. 81-85.

For a possible exception, in which the daughter of Ibal-Addu, a *šugītum*, may have been taken prisoner in war and subsequently assigned to the textile factory, see above, chap. 6, p. 109.

CHAPTER 9

THE PROPHETESSES

The discovery of the existence of prophets and prophecy at Mari has in recent years occasioned much scholarly investigation of this phenomenon.[1] But despite a spate of monographs and articles, little attention has been paid to the specific role of women in this activity. The following treatment will concentrate on what can be gleaned from the Mari texts about the so-called prophetesses and the role of women in prophetic activity.

Initially, the prophetesses of Mari may be divided into two categories: professional prophetesses and lay prophetesses. Professional prophetesses include the female respondent (*āpiltum*), the female ecstatic (*muḫḫūtum*), and the female speaker (*qabbātum*). These women, like their male counterparts, are termed professionals because they were attached to a specific deity or temple and had as their function the communication of the will of that deity to others. They may have served in other capacities as well. The male ecstatic (*muḫḫum*) is definitely part of the temple personnel, as a ritual text for the cult of Ištar makes clear.[2] These professional prophets are as a rule designated by specifying the deity to which they were devoted: the *āpilum* of Adad of Kallassu/Ḫalad; the *aplûm* of Dagan of Tuttul; Qišti-Diritum, the *āpilum* of Diritum; the *āpilum* of Šamaš (in Sippar); the *muḫḫûm* of Dagan (in Terqa); the *muḫḫûm* of Dagan (in Tuttul); the *qabbātum* of Dagan of Terqa. Sometimes, however, reference is made to the temple instead: Iṣiaḫu, the *āpilum* in the temple of Ḫišametum; the *muḫḫūtum* in the temple of Annunitum. Consequently, it is of no significance when on a rare occasion no deity or temple is mentioned. In X 81.4 Innibana is merely identified as the *āpiltum*. Apparently she was well known to the king and did not need to be further identified. Moran[3] has convincingly shown that Innibana delivered her oracle in a temple--perhaps that of Annunitum--and was perhaps attached to that temple.

There seems to have been but one respondent, one ecstatic, and one speaker attached to any one god or temple. There is never mention of more than one of any given category for any god or temple. There is never mention of more than one of any given category for any god or temple. The fact that the professional prophet(ess)'s name is often omitted and simply referred to as "the respondent, etc., of god x" is to be taken as proof that the god had but one of these prophets; no further identification was needed. The lone exception to this generalization occurs in a letter of Nur-Sin[4] communicating an oracle from Adad of Ḫalab/Kallassu, which concludes with the statement:

> *an-ni-tam* LÚ.MEŠ *a-pí-lu iq-bu-ú ù i-na te-re-tim*
> *i-ta-na-az-za-az i-na-an-na ap-pu-na-ma*
> LÚ *a-*[*pí*]*-lum ša* ^{d}IM *be-el ka-al-la-sú*^{ki}
> *ma-aš-ka-nam ša a-la-aḫ-tim*^{ki} *a-na ni-iḫ-la-tim*$^{\{ki\}}$
> *i-na-aṣ-ṣa-ar*
>
> This is what the respondents said. And he is constantly appearing at (the inspection of) the omens. And now in addition the respondent of Adad the lord of Kallassu is guarding the threshing floor(?) of Alaḫatum as the hereditary property ("Lods," 24-28).[5]

The mention of "respondents" (plural) may be a mistake; in the next sentence the predicate is singular (*ittanazzaz*). If this is not a mistake, then it must be assumed that the shrine of Adad in Aleppo (Ḫalab) is distinct from that in Kallassu. They apparently were close together,[6] and the respondents of both shrines appear to have collaborated in a common oracle which each delivered at this own shrine. Thus the situation in Ḫalab/Kallassu does not differ from that observed elsewhere.

But while there may be but one each of any given category of professional prophet at a sanctuary, a single sanctuary may possess more than one kind of prophet. Thus Dagan of Terqa had a male ecstatic (*muḫḫûm*) and a female speaker(*qabbātum*); and Dagan of Tuttul had a male respondent (*aplûm*) and male ecstatic (*muḫḫûm*). And if Innibana is to be attached to the temple of Annunitum, as suggested above, then that temple

TABLE 3

PUBLIC AND PRIVATE PROPHECIES

Sex	Text	Subject	Prophetical Status
		Public Prophecies	
M	"Lods"	LÚ.MEŠ *āpilū*	pro
M	"	*āpilum ša* ^d^*Adad bēl Kallassu*	pro
M	{ "Lods" A.2925 }	*āpilum ša* ^d^*Adad bel Ḫalab*	pro
M	XIII 23	*aplûm ša* ^d^*Dagan ša Tut*[*tul*]	pro
M	X 53	Iṣiaḫu, *āpilum ina bīt* ^d^*Ḫišamētim*	pro
M	A.455	*muḫḫûm* (before Dagan in Tuttul)	pro
M	X 7	Šelibum, (*assinnum*) *ina bīt Annunītim immaḫū*	lay
F	{ X 50.22f. VI 45 }	*muḫḫūtum ina bīt Annunītim*	pro
F	X 81	Innibana, *āpiltum*	pro
F	X 8	Aḫatum, SAL.TUR *Dagan-mālik immaḫī*, *ina bīt Annunītim*	lay
		Private Prophecies	
M	{ II 90 III 40 }	*muḫḫûm ša* ^d^*Dagan* (in Terqa)	pro
M	III 78	*muḫḫûm* (of Dagan(?), in Terqa)	pro
M	X 9	Qišti-Diritim, *āpilum ša Dīrītim*	pro
M	A.4260	*āpilum* (of Šamaš, in Sippar)	pro
M	X 6	Ili-ḫasnaya, *assinnum ša An*[*nunītim*(?)]	lay
F	X 80	*qabbātum ša* ^d^*Dagan ša Terqa*	pro
F	XIII 114	*aššat awīlim*	lay
(F	X 100	Dan(?)-na-na	lay)

pro = professional

had both a female respondent and female ecstatic (*muḫḫūtum*).

It is perhaps only by chance that the Mari texts have preserved the record of but one female respondent (Innibana) while they mention a number of male respondents. Like their male counterparts, female respondents perhaps functioned at many temples. This would appear to be the implication of the remark by Nur-Sin:

> *pa-na-nu-um i-nu-ma i-na ma-ri*^{ki} *wa-aš-ba-ku*
> LÚ *a-pí-lum ù* ^{f}*a-pí-il-tum mi-im-ma a-wa-tam*
> *ša i-qa-*[*ab-bu-*]*nim a-na be-lí-ia ú-ta-ar*
>
> Previously when I resided in Mari, I would relay to my lord whatever message a prophet or a prophetess would say to me...("Lods" 29-31).

Not only were female respondents common, but they seem to have prophesied with as much frequency as their male counterparts.

The female ecstatic (*muḫḫutum*) is mentioned in two texts, X 50.22 and VI 45.9, 15. These two texts are, however, concerned with the same woman and the same event.[7] This female ecstatic was attached to the temple of Annunitum, where she delivered her oracle. The incident allows us a glimpse of the structure of temple prophets in Mari. The prophet(ess) was apparently free to give an oracle whenever the god so prompted. However, the prophet(ess) was not exempt from the control of the temple administrator (*šangûm*).[8] In this case Aḫum, the administrator of the Annunitum temple,[9] takes the legally required symbols after a public oracle and brings them to the governor of Mari so that they can be sent to the king (VI 45). As Aḫum proceeds similarly in the case of the ecstatic lay woman Aḫatum (X 8), it must be assumed that the temple administrator was responsible for all such activities within his domain. Prophets, professional and lay, were subject to his supervision and consequently their activities were carefully observed.

The oracle of the female speaker (*qabbātum*) of Dagan of Terqa is reported in X 80.6f. This woman surely resided and functioned in Terqa, as her title indicates. But she apparently traveled to Mari to deliver her message. Perhaps she had intended to personally deliver her message to the king. Not finding him there, she gave the message to Inib-šina to be forwarded to Zimri-Lim. Why this should have been necessary is not apparent. Certainly the governor of Terqa was capable of transmitting such an oracle to the king, as he did on other occasions. The circumstances surrounding this incident remain unclear.[10]

Just how the *qabbātum* differed from other kinds of prophets(esses) is unknown. She is not elsewhere attested. Her male counterpart is not mentioned in the Mari texts.[11]

When we turn to lay women, we find them represented in all types of prophetical activity at Mari. They may go into ecstasy in the temple and deliver a public oracle (X 8), or they may deliver their oracle privately (XIII 114; X 100). Most frequently, however, their prophetic experience is in the form of a dream (X 10;[12] 50; 94; 117). All levels of society are represented among lay women, although the higher the lay woman's position, the less likely she is to be involved in culturally unacceptable--by Babylonian standards--activities. Thus prophecy seems to have been a Western phenomenon which was ill received by the more sophisticated Babylonians; these latter relied chiefly upon the "science" of the haruspex.[13] Consequently, the fact that the lowly Aḫatum, the servant girl of one Dagan-malik,[14] went into ecstasy and prophesied occasioned no surprise. But on another occasion when a lay woman of some importance delivered an oracle, it was considered of particular significance. In reporting the incident, the governor of Terqa stresses the woman's high social status: "The wife of a free-man (*aššat awīlim*) came to me and spoke as follows..." (XIII 11f.8). The status of the prophetess was considered even more important than her name, which is omitted.[15] Dreams, on the other hand, were acceptable in Babylonian culture, and participation in this form of divinatory activity carried no special stigma. It is significant, then, that dreams were experienced even by such prominent persons as the temple administrator Iddin-ili, Malik-Dagan, the ruler of the city Sakka, and the women Addu-duri and Sibatum --the latter woman apparently a princess.[16]

By far the most common form of divine revelation experienced by lay persons, both menand women, was the dream.[17] By way of contrast, no professional prophet in these texts received his or her divine communication in a dream. Dreams did not require any technical skill, nor were they dependent upon one's status, hence their popularity among nonprofessional persons. Dreams were experienced with equal frequency by men and women. However, in conformity with a broader ancient Near Eastern pattern for dreams,[18] men tended to experience "message" dreams while women tended to experience "symbolic" dreams (i.e., dreams needing interpretation).[19]

TABLE 4

DREAMS

Sex	Text	Subject	Type
M	A.15	Malik-Dagan, *awīl Šakka*^{ki}	message
M	XIII 112	*ṣuḫārum*	message
M	XIII 113	*awīlum*	[message(?)]
M	X 51	Iddin-ili, *šangûm*	message
F	X 10	Kakkalidi	symbolic
F	X 50.3-21	Addu-duri	symbolic
F	X 94	Šibatum	[symbolic(?)]
F	X 117	Timlu	[?]

Conclusion

From the preceding it is clear that women participated equally in all types of prophetic activity, whether professional or lay, public or private. There were male respondents and female respondents, male ecstatics and female ecstatics, in addition to the female speaker (*qabbātum*). Women were as likely to receive divine revelations through dreams as were men.

The equal competency of women with men in communicating the will of the gods is explicitly confirmed by a remark of Šibtu. In a letter to her husband relating how she sought to determine the outcome of the impending battle between him and Išme-Dagan, she writes:

aš-šum ṭe$_4$*-em ge-er-ri-im*
ša be-lí i-la-ku it-ta-tim
zi-ka-ra-am ù sí-in-ni-iš-tam
ú!-qí áš-ta-al-ma i-ge-er-ru-ú-um
a-na be-lí-ia ma-di-iš da-mi-iq
a-na iš-me-^{d}*da-gan qa-tam-ma*
zi-ka-ra-am ù ⌜sí⌝-in-ni-iš-tam

10) *àš-ta-al-ma i-ge-er-ru-šu*
ú-ul da-mi-iq

For a report of the campaign which my lord is on, I waited(?)[20] on signs. I asked a man and a woman, and the word is very favorable to my lord. Similarly, with regard to Išme-Dagan I asked the man and the woman, and his prognosis is not favorable...(X 4.3-11).

The method the man and the woman employed to divine the will of the god(s) is not specified--it is not important. The emphasis is on the fact that both a man and a woman have been consulted and that they agree! Further on in the letter the queen emphatically stresses:

mi-im-ma ú-ul ⌜*ú-ša*⌝*-ad-ba-*[*ab-šu-nu-ti*]
šu-nu-ma i-da-ab-bu-bu šu-nu[*-ma*]
im-ta-ḫa-[*ru*]

I am not making them speak. On their own they speak; on their own they agree! (11. 37-39.

The agreement by a man and by a woman leaves no room for doubt about the veracity of the report.

This stress on the equal competency of a woman diviner stands in marked contrast to the normal Babylonian form of divination. In the latter, the craft of divination (*bārûtum*) was reserved to men, the *bārû*-priests). Within the Western heritage of Mari, however, other forms of divination were also operative which were notable for their lack of discrimination against women.

NOTES TO CHAPTER 9

THE PROPHETESSES

[1]The literature on the Mari prophets and prophecy is extensive and rapidly growing. Here only some of the more important (for our purposes) recent literature is cited: Dossin, "Sur le prophétisme à Mari," *Rencontre XIV*, 77-86; Ellermeier, *Prophetie in Mari und Israel* (Herzberg, 1968); Moran, "New Evidence from Mari on the History of Prophecy," *Biblica* 50 (1969), 15-56; P. R. Berger, "Einige Bemerkungen zu Ellermeier," *UF* I (1969), 207-9, 221; von Soden, Einige Bemerkungen zu Ellermeier," *UF* I, 198-99; Renger, *Priestertum* II, 218-23; Huffmon, *The Biblical Archaeologist* 31 (1968), 101-24. For older literature, the reader is referred to the bibliographies given in the works by Ellermeier and Moran cited in this note.

[2]Dossin, *RA* 35 (1938), 6, ii.22 and 8, iv.36. See further Huffmon, *The Biblical Archaeologist* 31 (1968), 112.

[3]*Biblica* 50, 25, n. 1, and 34.

[4]The name of the writer is missing for this text ("Lods"), but it may easily be supplied from another very similar letter (A.2925) sent by Nur-Sin, Zimri-Lim's envoy in Aleppo; see Dossin, "Prophétisme," 78.

[5]See Moran, *ANET*^{3}, 625.

[6]The exact location of Kallassu is unknown. It was very near to Aleppo, if not a quarter of the city itself; see Klengel, *JCS* 19 (1965), 89.

[7]See Moran, *Biblica* 50 (1969), 20.

[8]On the *šangûm*, see Renger, *Priestertum* II, 104-21.

[9]For Aḫum as the *šangûm* of the Annunitum temple, see Moran, *Biblica* 50 (1969), 20.

[10]Ellermeier, *Prophetie*, 77, cautions against concluding that in this instance the woman is necessarily acting on behalf of the god Dagan.

[11]It is not certain that the *qabbā'um* is to be connected with the *qabbātum*; see Renger, *Priestertum* II, 219, n. 1044; *AHw* 886: "Untersuchungsfürer (für Geflüchtete)"; Goetze, *AS* 16 215.

[12]With Huffmon, *The Biblical Archaeologist* 31 (1968), 118f., and Ellermeier, *Prophetie*, 91, I include X 10 under the heading of dreams, contrary to Moran, *Biblica* 50 (1969), 46, who maintains that Kakkalidi experienced a vision. Even though the word "dream" (*šuttum*) is not used here, the incident conforms in every other way to the dream experience: ^{f}*ka-ak-ka-li-di i-na* É ^{d}*i-túr-me-er i-mu-ur* "Kakkalidi saw in the temple of Itur-Mer ...." Dreams are normally "seen" (*amārum*, *naṭālum*); see Oppenheim, *The Interpretation of Dreams*, 226. *amārum* is used of dreams in these texts in X 50.5,12 and X 117.9. The scene for the dream is also the temple in A.15. There is, then, no compelling reason to introduce here the complications involved in positing a "vision."

[13]Oppenheim, *Ancient Mesopotamia*, 221-22; Moran, *Biblica* 50 (1969), 23-24.

[14]^{m} ^{f}*a-ḫa-tum* SAL.TUR ^{d}*da-gan-ma-lik*. Ellermeier, *Prophetie*, 60, suggests that *mārtum* "daughter," rather than the normal *ṣuḫārtum/ṣeḫḫertum*, may be intended by the sumerogram SAL.TUR. This is not impossible; see above,

chap. 2, n. 56, and also Finet, "Le ṣuḫarum à Mari," *Rencontre XVIII*, 65-72, esp. p. 66.

[15]Text X 100, although often included among the "prophetic" texts from Mari, is excluded from consideration here. In this text the woman Dan(?)-na-na does not seem to be the recipient of an unprovoked revelation from a god; the "oracle" rather appears to be the solicited response of Dagan to a wronged and defenseless woman who had sought help against her aggressor. Thus there may have been no "prophecy" involved; the form the deity's response took is not specified. See Ellermeier, *Prophetie*, 97 and 163; Moran, *Biblica* 50 (1969), 56. Huffmon, *The Biblical Archaeologist* 31 (1968), 116, understands this as a case of nonprophetic incubation; incubation, however, must be rejected on grammatical grounds.

[16]For Addu-duri and her office, see above, chap. 3, pp. 64-72; for Šibatum and her status, see above, chap. 2, pp. 44-47.

[17]See Huffmon, *The Biblical Archaeologist*, 116-20.

[18]See Oppenheim, *The Interpretation of Dreams*, 190 and 240.

[19]Oppenheim, *ibid.*, suggests that "this might be taken to indicate that they ["symbolic" dreams] stem from a different level of contact between the worlds of the gods and humans than the "message" dreams.

[20]For the reading *ú'-qí*, and it's proper position, see Berger, *UF* I (1969), 221; *AHw* 931 *quʾʾū(m)* 4b.

CHAPTER 10

WOMEN IN SACRIFICE AND PRAYER

The two remaining areas of religion in which women may be observed participating actively are the offering of sacrifice and praying to the god(s). The role of women in these two religious acts will be taken up in that order.

Sacrifice

The offering of sacrifice may be official or private in nature. Because the Mari texts come from the royal archives, the majority of occurrences mentioned in them concern the king offering sacrifice in the official cult.[1] The motive behind the official cultic sacrifice was not only to honor the god(s) but also to insure the safety or long life of the king (XIII 23.4-5) or to seek some similar favor from the gods. The king often delegated the performance of this duty to one of his officers. It was in this capacity that the queen[2] and Addu-duri[3] offered sacrifice.

Women are also recorded as participating in private sacrifice. A private act of sacrifice is proposed by the author of X 113, undoubtedly Kiru,[4] the daughter of Zimri-Lim, who wished to go to Mari for that purpose. Thus she sought permission from her father to leave her post *lu-ul-li-ka-am-ma a-na* DINGIR.MEŠ *ša a-bi-ia ni-*⌈*q*⌉*é-em lu-uq-qí* "so that I may go and offer sacrifice to the gods of my father" (X 113.20-22). Šattamkiyazi also offered sacrifice. This woman was at one time part of the personnel of the royal "house" in Terqa,[5] but in X 87 she is in Sagaratum on assignment from the king. This assignment had been contrary to the will of her goddess, Ištara-danna, as expressed in the liver omens of the sacrifice that Šattamkiyazi had offered before the goddess (X 87.5f.).[6] As a consequence she has since been gravely ill in Sagaratum. Therefore she now requests permission to correct this dereliction by going and offering sacrifice to her goddess anew (ll. 24-30).

In the Assyrian period, Išḫi-Addu, king of Qatna, wrote to his son-in-law Yasmaḫ-Addu to come to him and bring along his wife, Išḫi-Addu's daughter, "so that she may appease (*lisallim*) the gods of her (native) city" (II 51.19-20). The action of appeasement consisted, no doubt, in offering sacrifice to the gods of Qatna.[7]

In an unusual transaction, Ištar-tappi, the daughter of Yaḫdun-Lim,[8] borrows money from the Šamaš temple. But instead of paying interest in silver, this princess is to sacrifice (*iṭabbaḫ*) two rams; the rams may be regarded as the equivalent of interest, however, since the offering would be used to sustain the temple personnel.

These instances of individual women offering sacrifice are not to be construed as attesting to any special status on the part of the woman who offers sacrifice. Rather they were pious acts incumbent upon every person toward his or her god(s).[9]

Prayer

Another religious activity in which women are frequently engaged is prayer. Although the percentage of documents which stem from women at Mari is small, women are more frequently portrayed as praying for others than are men. It would appear that, as in some modern Western cultures, the practice of personal acts of religion was believed to be more properly the role of women than of men.

The likelihood of this assumption is supported by the fact that, as in the case of the *nadītum* Erišti-Aya, the king's official representative who prayed for him before the deity was always a woman. The *nadiātum* often allude to their role as the prayer women of their benefactor (*kāribtaka*). But they were not the only women who fulfilled this function. In the Assyrian interregnum at Mari, Yasmaḫ-Addu received a letter from Kunšimatum in Terqa reminding him of her importance as his prayer woman, *a-na-ku ka-ri-ib-ta-ka* I[GI ^{d}]*da-gan* "I am your prayer woman before Dagan" (X 3.10′). The similarity of Kunšimatum's words to those of Erišti-Aya and other *nadiātum* suggests that Kunšimatum did have some kind of special commission as Yasmaḫ-Addu's official prayer woman before Dagan. But if our reconstruction of this woman's function as a secondary wife of the king is correct,[10] she apparently is merely expressing a somewhat exaggerated form of the prayer for the king enunciated by other women. Gabiatum also writes Yasmaḫ-Addu in similar, if somewhat less official-sounding, words: *a-na* ^{d}UTU *ù* ^{d}*d*[*a-gan*] *ak-ta-na-r*[*a-*]*ba-ku*[*m-ma*] "I am constantly praying for you to Šamaš and D[agan]" (X 1.5-6). And later, in the reign of Zimri-Lim, the women Šewirum-ubirit and Attukki inform the king that *šu-lum-ka u*[*r-ra-*]*am ù mu-ša-am ni-*[*k*]*a-ra-ba-k*[*u*]*m* "Day and night we pray for you" (X 93.17-18); but as this incident may involve a motive of gratitude, it is perhaps best taken up with a group of prayers which will be treated shortly. Although women are most frequently observed as the ones who pray for the king, men can and do sometimes perform this duty. Thus Kibri-Dagan, the governor of Terqa, informed his king of a pious act by the elders of his city: *ka-a-ia-an-tam* LÚ.MEŠ ŠU.GI *a-lim*^{ki} *a-na* IGI ^{d}*da-gan i-ru-bu-ma a-na be-lí-ia ù um-ma-na-tim ša be-lí-ia ú-ka-ar-ra-bu* "The elders of the city are constantly coming before Dagan and praying for my lord and the army of my lord" (III 17.17-20).

If the fact of prayer is often recorded, the actual words of the prayer are seldom included. At most, a summary of the prayer is given. This practice conforms to the usual practice in Mesopotamia.[11] Kunšimatum, in one of the rare summaries of the content, tells for what she prays:

an-na-tu-um ša IGI ^{d}*d*[*a-g*]*an*
ak-ta-na-ra-ba-[*k*]*u-um*
20´) *un-ma-mi* [^{m}*ia-ás-m*]*a-aḫ-*^{d}IM
lu ša-li-im-ma
ù a-na-ku i-na ṣí-i[*l-l*]*i-šu*
lu-dam-mi-iq

This is what I constantly pray before Dagan for you: "Let all be well with Yasmaḫ-Addu that I for my part may prosper under his protection" (X 3.18-23).[12]

Elsewhere only greeting formulae in the form of a prayer are given.[13] The characteristic greeting of the *nadītum* has already been discussed.[14] Similar pious greetings are found in the letters of Zimri-Lim's secondary wife to her husband: ^{d}*da-gan be-el ter-qa*^{ki} *a-ia-bi-ka ù na-ak-ri-ka a-na qa-ti-ka li-ma-li-ma* "May Dagan, the lord of Terqa, deliver your enemies and your foes into your hands" (X 62.9-12); Itur-Mer, "the king of Mari," is included with Dagan in other formulae: ^{d}*da-gan b*[*e-*]*el pa-ag-re-e ù* ^{d}*i-túr-me-er* LUGAL *ma-ri*^{ki} *a-ia-bi-ka ù na-a*[*k*]*-ri-ka* ⌜*a-na*⌝ *qa-t*[*i*]*-ka* [*li-ma-*]*lu-ú* "May Dagan, the lord of the dead(?) and Itur-Mer, the king of Mari, deliver your enemies and your foes into your hands" (X 63.15-19; cf. 66.16f.). Outside of letters to the king, Inib-šarri expressed a pious sentiment in her letter to her brother, Šunuḫraḫalu: *i-na ma-za-zi-ka* ^{d}NI[N.]⌜É⌝.GAL ⌜*li*⌝*-iṣ-ṣú-ur-ka* "May Belet-ekallim preserve you in your office" (X 78.7-8). Men at Mari used such greeting formulae with far less frequency than women: *aš-šu-mi-ia* ^{d}UTU *ù* <*i*>*-túr-me-er da-ri-iš i-na li-ib-bi a-li-im ma-ri*^{ki} *li-ṣú-ru-ka ù li-ba-li-ṭú-ka* "For my sake may Šamaš and Itur-Mer permanently guard you in the midst of Mari and preserve your life" (XIII 101.3-5). Somewhat different is the greeting which Dadi-Ḫadun uses in his letter to the queen: *ki-ma a-na-ku a-bu-ut-ki aṣ-ba-tu* ^{d}UTU *a-bu-ut a-wa-ti-ia li-iṣ-ba-at* "Just as I intercede on your behalf, may Samas intercede on behalf of my words" (X 156.30-33).

Occasionally the object of the prayer is someone other than the king. In this vein, the palace servant girls (*ṣeḫḫerētum*) tell the male palace servants (*gerseqqū*) "their brothers": *a-na* ^{d}NIN.É.GAL [*k*]*a-ia-ni-iš* [*n*]*i-uk*(sic!)*-ta-na-rá-ba-*[*k*]*u-*[*n*]*u-ši* "We are constantly praying for you to Belet-ekallim" (X 112.16-18). Undoubtedly, we would have many more examples of prayers for persons other than the king if we possessed more private letters.[15]

These prayers did not always spring from the noblest of motives, however. Often the author of a letter made no bones about his self-interest; his or her prayer was contingent upon receiving a favor. The writer says in no uncertain terms, Do this favor which I ask and I will bless you before god so-and-so. This kind of statement is encountered but once in a letter from a woman. Šewirum-ubrat claims that her governess has been unjustly taken from her and she appeals to the king: ^{f}*ta-ri-ti id-nam-ma ma-ḫa-ar* ^{d}IM *ù* ^{d}*ḫé-bat lu-uk-ru-ba-kum* "Give my governess back to me so that I may bless you before Tešub and Ḫebat" (X 92.21-23).[16]

Throughout the OB period, however, prayer in gratitude for a favor granted is found frequently in other contexts.[17] The king of Qatna, Išḫi-Addu, requests Yasmaḫ-Addu to join him in a military undertaking, suggesting that Yasmaḫ-Addu will be able to provide his troops with much booty and that they in turn will bless their king out of gratitude.[18] A similar psychology lies behind Išar-Lim's request of Yasmaḫ-Addu that the king give him a servant skilled in the art of fattening livestock, adding, "should I see (this), I would pray for my lord" (V 46.8-11).

From one point of view, these prayers with their accompanying promise of grateful blessing may be understood as simply the polite way in that culture of phrasing a request. It would thus be the equivalent of our "please." But from another point of view, these formulations reveal something of the religious psychology of the day. The petitioner requests the god(s) to do what he is not able to do, namely repay his benefactor with suitable good fortune.

The reverse side of the gratitude motive is the threat of the curse. If one blesses his benefactor for granting a favor, he may curse him for not granting the favor.[19] Although it is hardly expressed in so many words, both the petitioner and his would-be benefactor were aware of this implied threat. If a blessing was desirable, a curse was to be avoided at all costs. Taken together, the promise of a blessing and the threat of a curse served as a powerful inducement to grant the requested boon.

Conclusion

In the areas of sacrifice and prayer, the role of women cannot be especially distinguished from that of men. Both female and male deputies may conduct the official sacrifice. And if private women need permission to offer their sacrifices, it is only because their dependent status as a servant, or the like, does not allow them to travel to the place of sacrifice without the permission of their master. In the area of prayer women again participate as fully as men. Indeed, there is some evidence that the duty of prayer may have been ascribed more frequently to women than to men. At least the officially designated prayer representatives of the king were always women.

NOTES TO CHAPTER 10

WOMEN IN SACRIFICE AND PRAYER

[1]Such sacrifices are recorded for the reign of Yaḫdun-Lim (*Syria* 32, 13, 8-11), Šamši-Adad (I 10.13′), Yasmaḫ-Addu (IV 59.5f.; V 25.5, 15; 65.30f.; 75.12′), Zimri-Lim (II 90.17f., 97.18; III 45.15f.; VI 30.29; 74; *et passim*). Materials for such sacrifices provided from the royal stores are frequently documented; See Bottéro, *ARMT* VII, 193f., 341f.; Birot, *ARMT* IX, 349f.; *ARMT* XII, 23f.; Burke, *ARMT* XI, 141f.

[2]See above, chap. 1, p. 18.

[3]See above, chap. 3., pp. 67-68.

[4]On the ascription of this letter to Kiru, see above, chap. 2, p. 43.

[5]IX 25.24, 47 = 26.27′, r 19′; see Birot, *ARMT* IX, 331, no. 129.

[6]For this letter, see Römer, *Frauenbriefe*, 31; Roberts, *VT* 21 (1971), 246f.

[7]"Incidently, this text, and, for that matter, the above-quoted ARM 10 113: 17-22, make it clear that a princess' cultic duty before her native city's gods does not terminate with her marriage to a foreign ruler" (Sasson, "Royal Ladies," 77).

[8]See chap. 2, p. 51, with n. 53.

[9]See, for example, *BWL* 104, 135-45, which counsels daily worship through sacrifice and prayer; see also 109, 12.

[10]See above, chap. 1, pp.

[11]"Meist wurde nur die Tatsache des Gebets erwähnt, in anderen Fällen eine kurze Zusammenfassung des Inhalts gegeben" (von Soden, *RLA* III, 163a).

[12]See further above, chap. 1, pp. 24-25.

[13]See E. Salonen, *StOr* 38, 20f.

[14]See above, chap. 5, pp. 93-94.

[15]Von Soden, *RLA* III, 161b, expresses the opinion that prayer for anyone other than the king is a rare occurrence. However, this is not true, at least in the OB period; see, for example, VAB 6 181:23; 161:10; 116:14-17; *ABPh* 120:12; 27:23; TCL 17, 29:30-31; BIN 7, 44:29. In addition, one could cite many examples of *nadiātum* praying for their fathers: *ABPh* 60: 28, 105:13-15; 106:8-10, etc.; or for a brother: VAB 6 180:21. See also *CAD* K 196 *karābu* 3a 2′.

[16]This same woman (var. Šewirum-birit), in conjunction with another woman, Attukki, seemingly brings in the gratitude motive in another (damaged) letter (X 93.17-18); see above, p. 130.

[17]See, for example, VAB 6 116, 17; 120, 12; 180, 21; 240, 35; 238, 71; *ABPh* 27, 27; 104, 12; 119, 26; 120, 12; UCP 9, 339; *CT* 43 15, 29.

[18]*ṣa-ba-ka ša-al-la-tam šu-ki-il-ma ù li-ik-ru-bu-ni-kum* (V 16.11-13).

[19]The concept of blessing someone for a favor done but cursing him for an offense is common throughout the ancient Near East. The Old Testament contains a good example of this two-edged character of an action. The return of a poor man's pledged garment at sundown, since it constitutes a favor, will evoke the poor man's blessing (Dt 24:13) whereas retaining

it will make one susceptible to his curse (Ex 22: 25-27 [Heb. 24-26]). Other examples of blessing someone for a good turn can be found in Ps 72: 15 and Job 31: 20. The related concept of cursing someone for an offense is evident in 1 K 8: 31f; cf. Job 31: 30; see further, J. Scharbert, "'Fluchen' und 'Segnen' im Alten Testament," *Biblica* 39 (1958), 1-26. For an example in Akkadian literature of cursing someone for an injustice, see *BWL* 132, 112-15. "The Poor Man of Nippur" (see Gurney, *Anatolian Studies* 6 [1956], 145-62) aptly illustrates the concept of repaying the offense of one who has not only refused a poor man's request but who has heaped injury upon him to boot; the gods are not invoked in this case because the poor man was himself able to inflict ill fortune upon his oppressor. The gravity of the act takes on added significance when the object of the action is a poor, defenseless person; see F. C. Fensham, "Widow, Orphan, and the Poor in Ancient Near Eastern Legal and Wisdom Literature," *JNES* 21(1962), 129-39.

CONCLUSION

Since each of the preceding chapters was concluded with a summary of its contents, it is unnecessary to summarize further. Here we confine ourselves to some remarks suggested by these studies as a whole.

It will be recalled that most of the evidence which we have considered derived from the reign of Zimri-Lim; materials pertaining to women from other periods were sporadic and inconclusive. The records from periods prior to Zimri-Lim, being more remote, were probably deliberately disposed of by subsequent rulers. Additionally, during the Assyrian interregnum Mari was but a provincial capital, so that many state documents would not have been stored there, while under the independent Zimri-Lim Mari served as the central archives of the realm. Although substantial, these factors do not account for the whole difference. Zimri-Lim seems to have been personally more open to women. Almost by deliberate policy he accorded an unusual amount of power to the women of the royal family. Šibtu may well have been the single most powerful person in Mari after the king. If, as I have argued, the queen did function in effect as the king's personal representative at the capital during the king's frequent absences, she must have been able personally to challenge the jurisdiction of any official, even the governor. Within their own spheres Zimri-Lim's daughters played equally prestious roles.

We have suggested that influence, whether with the king or some other ranking individual, is the key in many, if not most, instances to the power of the royal women of Mari. Rarely does their power seem to be simply a matter of holding an office or possessing an official title. Even in those instances when we can determine or assign a title that factor alone does not constitute the power of the particular women.

Thus it was apparently not any institutionalized role of queenship *per se* but intimacy and prestige with the king that gave Šibtu her prepotency. Of course being queen gave Šibtu the opportunity to acquire that prestige and influence. We do not know Zimri-Lim's motive for tapping Inibšina, but it seems unlikely that her being the governor's wife was the sole reason. More likely, her position allowed her to catch the king's eye. This is not to say that official status was not a factor in a woman's power. Incumbency in an office greatly increased a woman's authority, as the case of Kiru as mayor in Ilanṣura illustrates. But even Kiru surely obtained her official position primarily on the strength of her relation to the king rather than because of her native ability.

Office and ability were far from being inoperative, to be sure. Especially for women outside the royal family, these factors must have been quite important. One has only to recall the pervasive roles of Addu-duri for an illustration of the power and influence that an office and/or ability could confer on a woman. Such women were rare, however. Normally functionaries were men: the governors, the *bārûm*-priests, who in addition to their divinatory duties served as commanders or other provincial leaders,[1] the controllers, the archivists, and others. An Addu-duri or, in a lesser capacity, an Ama-dugga is an exception to the rule.

There can be no doubt that men were culturally dominant. Thankful as we are for the feminine correspondence, by no stretch of the imagination can it approach, either in volume or in importance, the male correspondence. Even the administrative texts, apart from lists of captives and menial servants, deal for the most part with men and their functionaries. In addition, a cultural bias against women is revealed by incidental disparaging remarks sprinkled throughout these texts about the weak, unheroic character of women and by such statements as "Even though I am but a woman..." (X 31.7´-9´). In the matter of male dominance, Mari was in accord with the general Mesopotamian culture. The surprising fact, then, is not that women were regarded as inferior but that they were able to attain the great prominence that they did.

This political prominence of women in Mari and upper Mesopotamia stands in contrast both to their role in succeeding periods in Mesopotamian history and to the role of their contemporaries in lower Mesopotamia. This difference may be attributed to a different attitude toward women in the Western or Amorite culture which predominated in the royal circles of

Mari and northern Mesopotamia.

Although Mari had a long history of contact with the great city-state cultures of Sumer and Babylonia, its society remained dimorphic.[2] Throughout this region nomadism and sedentarism, tribe and town, existed in symbiotic tension. Reflective of this situation, Mari statecraft seems to have had less affinity with the classical culture of southern Mesopotamia than with the Amorite culture of the west. The "Lim dynasty" in particular remembered its roots in the tribe of Ḫana (see VI 76.20). The Assyrian house of Šamši-Adad had a similar history. Only recently emerged from the tribal stage, these Amorite rulers retained many of the features of their tribal heritage in their nascent political economies. In contrast to the developed city-states with their more clearly demarcated and institutionalized offices and chains of command, the northern Amorite kings seem to have retained a "patriarchal" type of rule. All authority was retained in the hands of the king, who personally oversaw all operations or at least personally delegated that authority as need required. The situation was similar in early monarchial Israel during the transition from tribal rule to incipient statecraft. There, too, personal influence with the king was of paramount importance for achieving power. This was applicable to men and women equally. One need only recall the influence of a Bathsheba on a David to get an inkling of the power a woman could acquire under such circumstances. It is not surprising, then, that in Amorite Mari some women, particularly the intimates of the king, achieved the prominence we have witnessed.

In our assessment of women exercising authority, it should be noted that at Mari there does not seem to have been any cultural barrier to women attaining and holding positions of equality with or even dominance over men either on a *de jure* or on a *de facto* level. This is evident in many examples from the area we have designated as politics. This interpretation is supported also by the economic texts, where women, though in far lesser numbers, appear alongside men, who, as vassals or other officials, contribute gifts to the king's coffers.[3] Some of these contributions may have been a kind of tax; others were munificence designed to secure a favorable standing with the king. Whatever the motive, women appear among the contributors in the same capacity as men.

Our studies of the religious sphere have shown that here, too, women suffered no institutionalized incapacity. Whether at the level of official cult or private devotion, women could and did function in ways equal to those of men. This was particularly true among the so-called prophets, where the messages of men prophets and women prophets were accorded equal worth. It is perhaps worth mentioning again that this non-Babylonian feature has likewise been attributed to a Western mentality.

In this study we have dealt for the most part with *les grandes dames* of Mari society. We should not forget, however, that these women were hardly typical of that society as a whole. Other texts reveal that the fortunes of the lowest classes, namely, the slaves and menial servants, were not nearly so agreeable. A multicolumned list of predominantly female captives (XIII 1) uprooted from their native towns and deported to Mari for work in the royal textile factories and other menial tasks is but one indication of the lot of women at the other end of the social scale. Nevertheless, there is no reason to believe that women were discriminated against in this regard. Other texts show that men suffered a similar lot.[4] At the bottom of every social scale, it mattered little whether a slave was male or female, except perhaps for determining the task to which he or she was to be assigned.

Little consideration has been given to those multitudes of Mari society who fall outside the pale of the palace. As is to be expected, these royal archives hardly concern themselves with such persons. Lacking documentation for such a vast segment of the population, every judgment is tenuous at best.

Despite these reservations, we believe that future research into the role and status of women at Mari--and much yet remains to be done--will confirm the outlines already sketched in this work and others. The picture which is emerging is, in terms of the Ancient Near East, very favorable to the women in that society. Lamentably, the cultural standing of women deteriorated in succeeding periods of Mesopotamian history. But while Mari flourished, women seemingly enjoyed a period of relative dignity and prominence.

NOTES TO CONCLUSION

[1]On the functions of the *bārûm*-priest at Mari, see Finet, "La place du devin dans la société de Mari," *Rencontre XIV*, 87-93; Renger, *Priestertum* II, 203-17.

[2]See Rowton's series of articles now appearing, as stated in "Urban Autonomy in a Nomadic Environment," *JNES* 32 (1973), 201-15; "Autonomy and Nomadism in Western Asia," *Or* 42 (1973), 247-58.

[3]In addition to women cited in the foregoing chapters, note also Partum (VII 91.5), Inib-šarri (VII 125; 203.1), Yakuttum(?) (VII 203.7´), Karanatum (VII 228), Rimatum (IX 253.i.17), Admubalaṭi (IX 253.ii.9), Ribatum (IX 258.4,6), Kimatum(?) (IX 280.7), Bele[t-] and Tebir-[ ] (VII 123.12-13).

[4]See the lists of menial workers, who undoubtedly were predominantly war slaves, given by Birot, *ARMT* IX, 331-43; see also Bottéro, *ARMT* VII, 216-17.

BIBLIOGRAPHY

Books and Pamphlets

Alexander, John Bruce. *Early Babylonian Letters and Economic Texts.* Babylonian Inscriptions in the Collection of James B. Nies, Yale University, VII. New Haven, 1943.

Bezold, Carl. *Babylonisch-assyrisches Glossar.* Heidelberg, 1926.

Birot, Maurice. *Archives royales de Mari, IX: Textes administratifs de la salle 5.* Musée du Louvre, Département des Antiquités Orientales, Textes cunéiformes, XXX. Paris, 1960.

________. *Archives royales de Mari, IX: Textes administratifs de la salle 5 du palais, transcrits, traduits et commentés.* Paris, 1960.

________. *Archives royales de Mari, XII: Texts administratifs de la salle 5 du palais (2ème Partie).* Paris, 1964.

Bottéro, Jean. *Archives royales de Mari, VII: Textes administratifs de la salle 110.* Musée du Louvre, Département des Antiquités Orientales, Textes cunéiformes, XXVIII. Paris, 1956.

________. *Archives royales de Mari, VII: Textes économiques et administratifs.* Paris, 1957.

________, and Finet, André. *Archives royales de Mari, XV: Répertoire analytique des tomes I à V.* Paris, 1954.

Boyer, Georges. *Archives royales de Mari, VIII: Textes juridiques et administratifs.* Musée du Louvre, Département des Antiquités Orientales, Textes cunéiformes, XXXIX. Paris, 1957.

________. *Archives royales de Mari, VIII: Textes juridiques, transcripts, traduits et commentés.* Paris, 1958.

Burke, Madeleine Lurton. *Archives royales de Mari, XI: Textes administratifs de la salle 111 du palais, transcrits, traduits et commentés.* Paris, 1963.

Cagni, Luigi. *L'Epopea di Erra.* Studi Semitici, 34. Roma, 1969.

Chiera, Edward. *Sumerian Religious Texts.* Upland, Pa., 1924.

Civil, Miguel, ed. *The Series lú = ša and Related Texts.* Materials for the Sumerian Lexicon, XII. Roma, 1969.

Dossin, Georges. *Lettres de la première dynastie babylonienne.* Musée du

Louvre, Département des Antiquités Orientales, Textes cunéiformes, XVII. Paris, 1933.

________. *Archives royales de Mari, I: Lettres*. Musée du Louvre, Département des Antiquités Orientales, Textes cunéiformes, XXII. Paris, 1946.

________. *Archives royales de Mari, I: Correspondance de Šamši-Addu et de ses fils, transcrite et traduite*. Paris, 1950.

________. *Archives royales de Mari, IV: Lettres*. Musée du Louvre, Département des Antiquités Orientales, Textes cunéiformes, XXV. Paris, 1951.

________. *Archives royales de Mari, IV: Correspondance de Šamši-Addu et de ses fils (suite), transcrite et traduite*. Paris, 1951

________. *Archives royales de Mari, V: Lettres*. Musée du Louvre, Département des Antiquités Orientales, Textes cunéiformes, XXVI. Paris, 1951.

________. *Archives royales de Mari, V: Correspondance de Iasmaḫ-Addu, transcrite et traduite*. Paris, 1952.

________. *Archives royales de Mari, X: La correspondance féminine*. Musée du Louvre, Département des Antiquités Orientales, Textes cunéiformes, XXXI. Paris, 1967.

________, *et al. Archives royales de Mari, XIII: Textes divers, transcrits, traduits et commentés*. Paris, 1964.

Driver, Godfrey Rolles, and Miles, John C. *The Assyrian Laws, edited with Translation and Commentary*. Oxford, 1935.

Ebeling, Erich. *Keilschrifttexte aus Assur religiösen Inhalts*, Band I. Wissenschaftliche Veröffentlichungen der Deutschen Orient-Gesellschaft, 28. Leipzig, 1919.

________, and Meissner, Bruno, eds. *Reallexikon der Assyriologie (und vorderasiatischen Archaeologie)*. Berlin and Leipzig, 1932-.

Edzard, Dietz Otto. *Altbabylonische Rechts- und Wirtschaftsurkunden aus Tell ed-Der im Iraq Museum, Baghdad*. Bayerische Akademie der Wissenschaften, Phil.-Hist. Klasse, Abhandlungen, N.F. 72. München, 1970.

Ellermeier, Friedrich. *Prophetie in Mari und Israel*. Theologische und orientalistische Arbeiten, 1. Herzberg, 1968.

Figulla, Hugo Heinrich. *Cuneiform Texts from Babylonian Tablets in the British Museum, Part XLIII: Old Babylonian Letters*. London, 1963.

________, and Martin, William J. *Ur Excavations, Texts, V: Letters and Documents of the Old-Babylonian Period*. London, 1953.

Finet, André. *L'Accadien des lettres de Mari*. Académie Royale de Belgique, Classe des lettres et des sciences morales et politiques, Mémoires, LX/1. Bruxelles, 1956.

Fish, Thomas. *Letters of the First Babylonian Dynasty (in the John Rylands Library)*. Manchester, 1936. (Also in *Bulletin of the John Rylands Library*, 16 [1932], 507-28, and 17 [1933], 106-20.)

Folkers, Th., *et al.*, eds. *Symbolae ad jura orientis antiqui pertinentes Paulo Koschaker dedicatae*. Studia et Documenta ad jura orientis antiqui pertinentia, II. Leiden, 1939.

Hallo, William W., and Simpson, William Kelly. *The Ancient Near East: A History*. New York, 1971.

Hallo, William W., and van Dijk, J. J. A. *The Exaltation of Inanna*. Yale Near Eastern Researches, 3. New Haven, 1968.

Harper, Robert Francis. *Assyrian and Babylonian Letters Belonging to the Kouyunjik Collection of the British Museum I-XIV*. London and Chicago, 1892-1914.

Hirsch, Hans. *Untersuchungen zur altassyrischen Religion*. Archiv für Orientforschung, Beiheft 13/14. Graz, 1961.

Huffmon, Herbert Bardwell. *Amorite Personal Names in the Mari Texts: A Structural and Lexical Study*. Baltimore, 1965.

Jacobsen, Thorkild. *The Sumerian King List*. Assyriological Studies, 11. Chicago, 1939.

Jean, Charles-F. *Archives royales de Mari, II: Lettres*. Musée du Louvre, Département des Antiquites Orientales, Textes cunéiformes, XXIII. Paris, 1941.

________. *Archives royales de Mari, II: Lettres diverse, transcrites et traduites*. Paris, 1950.

Kraus, Fritz Rudolf. *Briefe aus dem British Museum (CT 43 und 44)*. Altbabylonische Briefe in Umschrift und Übersetzung, Heft 1. Leiden, 1965.

Kupper, Jean-Robert. *Archives royales de Mari, III: Lettres*. Musée du Louvre, Département des Antiquités Orientales, Textes cunéiformes, XXIV. Paris, 1948.

________. *Archives royales de Mari, III: Correspondance de Kibri-Dagan, gouverneur de Terqa, transcrite et traduite*. Paris, 1950.

________. *Archives royales de Mari, VI: Lettres*. Musée du Louvre, Département des Antiquités Orientales, Textes cunéiformes, XXVII. Paris, 1953.

________. *Archives royales de Mari, VI: Correspondance de Baḫdi-Lim, préfet du palais de Mari, transcrite et traduite*. Paris, 1954.

________. *Les nomades en Mésopotamie au temps des rois de Mari*. Bibliothèque de la Faculté de Philosophie et Lettres du l'Université de Liège, CXLII. Paris, 1957.

Laessøe, Jørgen. *The Shemshāra Tablets: A Preliminary Report*. Arkaeol.-kunsthist. Medd. Dan. Vid. Selsk., IV/3. Copenhagen, 1959.

Lambert, Wilfred G. *Babylonian Wisdom Literature*. Oxford, 1967.

________, and Millard, A. R. *Cuneiform Texts from Babylonian Tablets in the British Museum, Part XLVI: Babylonian Literary Texts*. London, 1965

________. *Atra-ḫasīs: The Babylonian Story of the Flood*. Oxford, 1969.

Landsberger, Benno. *Der kultische-Kalender der Babylonier und Assyrer*. Leipziger Semitistische Studien, 6 I/II. Leipzig, 1915.

Lewy, Julius. *Tablettes cappadociennes, troisième série*. Deuxième partie. Musée du Louvre, Département des Antiquités Orientales, Textes cunéiformes, XX. Paris, 1936.

Lutz, Henry Frederick. *Early Babylonian Letters from Larsa.* Yale Oriental Series, Babylonian Texts, II. New Haven, 1917.

________. *Old Babylonian Letters.* University of California Publications in Semitic Philology, 9/4. Berkeley, 1929.

Meier, Gerhard. *Die assyrische Beschwörungssammlung Maqlû.* Archiv für Orientforschung, Beiheft 2. Berlin, 1937.

Meissner, Bruno. *Babylonien und Assyrien,* I-II. Heidelberg, 1920-25.

Oppenheim, A. Leo. *The Interpretation of Dreams in the Ancient Near East.* Transactions of the American Philosophical Society, 46/3 (1956), 179-373.

________. *Ancient Mesopotamia: Portrait of a Dead Civilization.* Chicago, 1964.

________. *Letters from Mesopotamia.* Chicago, 1967.

________, *et al.*, eds. *The Assyrian Dictionary of the Oriental Institute of the University of Chicago.* Chicago, 1956-.

Parrot, André, ed. *Studia Mariana.* Documenta et Monumenta orientis antiqui, IV. Leiden, 1950.

________, *et al. Mission archéologique de Mari, II: Le palais,* 3 vols. Bibliothèque archéologique et historique, LXX. Paris, 1958-59.

Praag, A. van. *Droit matrimonial assyro-babylonien.* Amsterdam, 1945.

Römer, Willem H. Ph. *Frauenbriefe über Religion, Politik und Privatleben in Mari: Untersuchungen zu G. Dossin, Archives Royales de Mari X (Paris 1967).* Alter Orient und Altes Testament, 12. Neukirchen-Vluyn, 1971.

Salonen, Armas. *Die Wasserfahrzeuge in Babylonien nach šumerisch-akkadischen Quellen.* Studia Orientalia, VIII/4. Helsinki, 1939.

________. *Die Landfahrzeuge des alten Mesopotamien nach sumerisch-akkadischen Quellen.* Annales Academiae Scientiarum Fennicae, Ser. B, 72/3. Helsinki, 1951.

________. *Die Türen des alten Mesopotamien.* Annales Academiae Scientiarum Fennicae, Ser. B, 124. Helsinki, 1961.

Salonen, Erkki. *Die Gruss- und Höflichkeitsformeln in babylonisch-assyrischen Briefen.* Studia Orientalia, XXXVIII. Helsinki, 1967.

Schorr, M. *Urkunden des altbabylonischen Zivil- und Prozessrechts.* Vorderasiatische Bibliothek, 5. Leipzig, 1913.

Schroeder, Otto. *Altbabylonische Briefe.* Vorderasiatische Schriftdenkmäler der Königlichen Museen zu Berlin, 16. Leipzig, 1917.

Soden, Wolfram von. *Gundriss der akkadischen Grammatik.* Analecta Orientalia, 33. Roma, 1952.

________, ed. *Akkadisches Handwörterbuch, Unter Benutzung des lexikalischen Nachlasses von Bruno Meissner (1868-1947).* Wiesbaden, 1959-.

________. *Ergänzungsheft zum Grundriss der akkadischen Grammatik.* Analecta Orientalia, 47. Roma, 1969.

Spycket, Agnès. *Les statues de culte dans les textes mesopotamiens des origines à la 1re dynastie de Babylone.* Cahiers de la Revue biblique, 9. Paris, 1968.

Thompson, R. Campbell. *Cuneiform Texts from Babylonian Tablets, etc., in the British Museum, Part XVIII.* London, 1904.

Thureau-Dangin, François. *Lettres et contrats de l'epoque de la première dynastie babylonienne.* Musée du Louvre, Département des Antiquités Orientales, Textes cunéiformes, I. Paris, 1910.

Ungnad, Arthur. *Babylonische Briefe aus der Zeit der Ḫammurapi-Dynastie.* Vorderasiatische Bibliothek, 6. Leipzig, 1914.

________. *Babylonian Letters of the Ḫammurapi Period.* Publications of the Babylonian Section, University Museum, University of Pennsylvania, VII. Philadelphia, 1914.

________. *Altbabylonische Briefe aus dem Museum zu Philadelphia.* Stuttgart, 1920.

Waterman, Leroy. *Royal Correspondence of the Assyrian Empire I-IV.* Ann Arbor, 1930-36.

Articles

Artzi, P., and Malamat, A. "The Correspondence of Šibtu, Queen of Mari in ARM X," *Orientalia*, N.S. 40 (1971), 75-89.

Astour, Michael C. "Tamar the Hierodule: An Essay in the Method of Vestigial Motifs," *Journal of Biblical Literature*, 85 (1966), 185-96.

Berger, P.-R. "Einige Bemerkungen zu Friedrich Ellermeier: Prophetie in Mari und Israel (Herzberg 1968)," *Ugarit-Forschungen*, 1 (1969), 207-9.

________. "Nachtrag 2," *Ugarit-Forschungen*, 1 (1969), 221.

Birot, Maurice. "Textes économiques de Mari (IV)," *Revue d'assyriologie et d'archéologie orientale*, 50 (1956), 57-72.

________. "Un recensement de femmes au royaume de Mari," *Syria*, 35 (1958), 9-26.

________. "Les lettres de Iasîm-Sumû," *Syria*, 41 (1964), 25-65.

________. "Simaḫlane, roi de Kurda," *Revue d'assyriologie et d'archéologie orientale*, 66 (1972), 131-39.

Bottéro, Jean. "La femme dans l'Asie occidentale ancienne: Mésopotamie et Israël," in Pierre Grimal, ed., *Histoire mondiale de la femme. Préhistoire et antiquité*, pp. 153-247. Paris, 1956.

________. "Lettres de la salle 110 du palais de Mari," *Revue d'assyriologie et d'archéologie orientale*, 52 (1958), 163-76.

Civil, Miguel. "The 'Message of Lú-dingir-ra to His Mother' and a Group of Akkado-Hittite 'Proverbs,'" *Journal of Near Eastern Studies*, 23 (1964), 1-11.

Cooper, Jerrold S. "New Cuneiform Parallels to the Song of Songs," *Journal of Biblical Literature*, 90 (1971), 157-62.

Donner, H. "Art und Herkunft des Amtes der Königinmutter im Alten Testament," in R. von Kienle *et al.*, eds., *Festschrift Johannes Friedrich zum 65. Geburtstag am 27. August 1958 gewidmet*, pp. 105-45. Heidelberg, 1959.

Dossin, Georges, "Les archives épistolaires du palais de Mari," *Syria*, 19 (1938), 105-26.

________. "Un rituel de culte d'Ištar provenant de Mari," *Revue d'assyri-*

ologie et d'archéologie orientale, et (1938), 1-13.

________. "Les archives économiques du palais de Mari," *Syria*, 20 (1939), 97-113.

________. "Iamḫad et Qatanum," *Revue d'assyriologie et d'archéologie orientale*, 36 (1939), 46-54.

________. "Une mentione du Ḫattuša dans une lettre de Mari," *Revue Hittite et Asianique*, 35 (1939), 70-76.

________. "Une revelation de dieu Dagan à Terqa," *Revue d'assyriologie et d'archéologie orientale*, 42 (1948), 125-34.

________. "Šibtu, reine de Mari," *Actes du XXIe Congrès International des Orientalistes* (Paris, 23-31 juillet 1948), pp. 142-43. Paris, 1949.

________. "Le panthéon de Mari," in André Parrot, ed., *Studia Mariana*, pp. 41-50. Documenta et Monumenta orientis antiqui, IV. Leiden, 1950.

________. "Les noms d'années et d'éponymes dans les 'Archives de Mari,'" in André Parrot, ed., *Studia Mariana*, pp. 51-61. Documenta et Monumenta orientis antiqui, IV. Leiden, 1950.

________. "Le royaume d'Alep au XVIIIe siècle avant notre ère d'après les 'Archives de Mari,'" *Bulletin de l'Académie Royale de Belgique, Classe des lettres et des sciences morales et politiques*, Series 5, Vol. XXXVIII (1952), 229-39.

________. "Le royaume de Qatna au XVIIIe siècle avant notre ère d'après les 'Archives royales de Mari,'" *Bulletin de l'Académie Royale de Belgique, Classe des lettres et des sciences morales et politiques*, Series 5, Vol. XL (1954), 417-25.

________. "L'inscription de fondation de Jaḫdun-Lim, roi de Mari," *Syria*, 32 (1955), 1-28.

________. "L'ordalie à Mari," *Comptes rendus des séances de l'Académie des Inscriptions et Belles Lettres* (1958), 387-92.

________. "À propos de la tablette administrative de *A.R.M.T.*, XIII, N° 1," *Syria*, 41 (1964), 21-24.

________. "Sur le prophétisme à Mari," in *La divination en Mésopotamie ancienne et dans les régions voisines*, pp. 77-86. Compte rendu de la XIVe Rencontre Assyriologique Internationale (Strasbourg, 2-6 juillet 1965). Paris, 1966.

________. "Archives de Sûmu-Iamam, Roi de Mari," *Revue d'assyriologie et d'archéologie orientale*, 64 (1970), 17-44.

________. "La route de l'etain en Mésopotamie au temps de Zimri-Lim," *Revue d'assyriologie et d'archéologie orientale*, 64 (1970), 97-106.

________. "Le nom de signe '(m)ušlânu,'" *Revue d'assyriologie et d'archéologie orientale*, 64 (1970), 162-63.

________. "Une capture de lion au Ḫabour d'après une lettre de Mari," *Bulletin de l'Académie Royale de Belgique, Classe des lettres et des sciences morales et politiques*, Series 5, vol. LVI (1970), 307-20.

________. "Deux listes nominatives du règne de Sûmu-Iamam," *Revue d'assyriologie et d'archéologie orientale*, 65 (1971), 37-66.

________. "Documents de Mari," *Syria*, 48 (1971), 1-19.

________. "*Adaššum* et *kirḫum* dans des textes de Mari," *Revue d'assyriologie et d'archéologie orientale*, 66 (1972), 111-30.

Ebeling, Erich. "Ebabbara," in *Reallexikon der Assyriologie*, Band II, p. 263. Berlin and Leipzig, 1938.

Eilers, Wilhelm. *Semiramis: Entstehung und Nachhall einer altorientalischen Sage*. Österreichische Akademie der Wissenshaften, Phil.-Hist. Klasse 247, 2. Wien, 1971.

Falkenstein, Adam. "Zu den Inschriftfunden der Grabung in Uruk-Warka 1960-1961," *Baghdader Mitteilungen*, 2 (1963), 1-82.

Fensham, F. Charles. "Widow, Orphan, and the Poor in Ancient Near Eastern Legal and Wisdom Literature," *Journal of Near Eastern Studies*, 21 (1962), 129-39.

Finet, André. "Les medecins au royaume de Mari," *Annuaire de l'Institut de Philologie et d'Histoire Orientales et Slaves*, 14 (1954-57), 123-44.

________. "Une lettre de récriminations au vice-roi de Mari, Iasmaḫ-Addu," *Annuaire de l'Institut de Philologie et d'Histoire Orientales et Slaves*, 15 (1958-60), 17-32.

________. "Une affaire de disette dans un district du royaume de Mari," *Revue d'assyriologie et d'archéologie orientale*, 53 (1959), 57-69.

________. "Iawi-Ilâ, roi de Talḫayûn," *Syria*, 41 (1964), 117-42.

________. "La place du devin dans la société de Mari," in *La Divination en Mésopotamie ancienne et dans les régions voisines*, pp. 87-93. Compte rendu de la XIVe Rencontre Assyriologique Internationale (Strasbourg, 2-6 juillet 1965). Paris, 1966.

________. "Adalšeni, roi de Burundum," *Revue d'assyriologie et d'archéologie orientale*, 60 (1966), 17-28.

________. "Le ṣuḫarum à Mari," *Gesellschaftsklassen im Alten Zweistromland und in den angrenzenden Gebieten--XVIII Rencontre assyriologique internationale, München, 29. Juni bis 3. Juli 1970*. Herausgegeben von D. O. Edzard. Bayerische Akademie der Wissenschaften, Phil.-Hist. Klasse, Abhandlungen, N.F. 75 (1972), 65-72.

Gadd, Cyril John. "The Cities of Babylonia," in *The Cambridge Ancient History*, 3rd ed., Vol. I, part 2, pp. 93-144. Cambridge, 1971.

Garelli, Paul, and le Breton, Louis. "La Sixième Rencontre Assyriologique Internationale, Paris, 27-30 juin 1958, Compte rendu de travaux," *Bibliotheca Orientalis*, 13 (1956), 178-79.

Goetze, Albrecht. "Tavern Keepers and the Like in Ancient Babylonia," in Hans G. Gütterbock and Thorkild Jacobsen, eds., *Studies in Honor of Benno Landsberger on His Seventy-fifth Birthday*, pp. 211-15. Assyriological Studies, 16. Chicago, 1965.

Gurney, Oliver R. "The Sultantepe Tablets, V. The Tale of the Poor Man of Nippur," *Anatolian Studies*, 6 (1956), 145-62.

Harris, Rivkah. "Biographical Notes on the *nadītu* Women of Sippar," *Journal of Cuneiform Studies*, 16 (1962), 1-12.

________. "The Organization and Administration of the Cloister in Ancient

Babylonia," *Journal of the Economic and Social History of the Orient*, 6 (1963), 121-57.

________. "The *nadītu*-Woman," in *Studies Presented to A. Leo Oppenheim*, pp. 106-35. Chicago, 1964.

Huffmon, Herbert Bardwell. "Prophecy in the Mari Letters," *The Biblical Archaeologist*, 31 (1968), 101-24.

Jacobsen, Thorkild. "The Akkadian Ablative Accusative," *Journal of Near Eastern Studies*, 22 (1963), 18-29.

Jastrow, Morris. "Veiling in Ancient Assyria," *Revue archéologique*, V^{e} série, 14 (1921), 209-38.

Jean, Charles-F. "Lettres de Mari IV, transcrites et traduites," *Revue d'assyriologie et d'archéologie orientale*, 42 (1948), 53-78.

Klengel, Horst, "Zu den *šībūtum* in altbabylonischer Zeit," *Orientalia*, N.S. 29 (1960), 357-75.

________. "Die Rolle der 'Ältesten' (LÚ^{MEŠ}ŠU.GI) im Kleinasien der Hethiterzeit," *Zeitschrift für Assyriologie und vorderasiatische Archäologie*, 57/N.F. 23 (1965), 223-36.

________. "Der Wettergott von Ḫalab," *Journal of Cuneiform Studies*, 19 (1965), 87-93.

Klíma, Josef. "La vie sociale et économique à Mari," in *La Civilisation de Mari*, pp. 39-50. Compte rendu de la XVe Rencontre Assyriologique Internationale (Liège, 4-8 juillet 1966). Liège, 1967.

Korošec, Viktor. "Les relations internationales d'après les lettres de Mari," in *La Civilisation de Mari*, pp. 139-50. Compte rendu de la XVe Rencontre Assyriologique Internationale (Liège, 4-8 juillet 1966). Liège, 1967.

Kraus, Fritz Rudolf. "Weitere Texte zur babylonischen Physiognomatik," *Orientalia*, N.S. 16 (1947), 172-205.

________. "'*ūmšum*' und Verwandtes," *Revue d'assyriologie et d'archéologie orientale*, 62 (1968), 77-79.

________. "Akkadische Wörter und Ausdrücke, I-III," *Revue d'assyriologie et d'archéologie orientale*, 64 (1970), 53-61.

________. "Akkadische Wörter und Ausdrücke, VI-VIII," *Revue d'assyriologie et d'archéologie orientale*, 65 (1971), 97-112.

Krecher, Joachim. "Göttersymbole und -attribute, B. Nach sumerischen und akkadischen Texten," in *Reallexikon der Assyriologie und vorderasiatischen Archaeologie*, Band III/7, pp. 495-98. Berlin, 1969.

Kupper, Jean-Robert. "Baḫdi-Lim, préfet du palais de Mari," *Bulletin de l'Académie Royale de Belgique, Classe des lettres et des sciences morales et politiques*, Series 5, Vol. XL (1954), 572-87.

________. "Sceaux-cylindres du temps de Zimri-Lim," *Revue d'assyriologie et d'archeologie orientale*, 53 (1959), 97-100.

________. "Correspondance de Kibri-Dagan," *Syria*, 41 (1964), 105-16.

Lambert, Maurice. "Les dieu~~x~~-vivants à l'aube des temps historiques," *Sumer*, 5 (1949), 8-33.

Landsberger, Benno. "Zu den Frauenklassen des Kodex Hammurabi," *Zeitschrift für Assyriologie und vorderasiatische Archaeologie*, 30 (1915-16), 67-73.

________. "Studien zu den Urkunden aus der Zeit des Ninurta-tukul-Aššur," *Archiv für Orientforschung*, 10 (1935), 140-59.

________. "Akkadisch-hebräische Wortgleichungen," in *Hebräische Wortforschung, Festschrift zum 80. Geburtstag von Walter Baumgartner*, pp. 176-204. *Vetus Testamentum*, Supplements, XVI. Leiden, 1967.

Lewy, Hildegard. "The Chronology of the Mari Texts," in *La Civilisation de Mari*, pp. 13-28. Compte rendu de la XVe Rencontre Assyriologique Internationale (Liége, 4-8 juillet 1966). Liége, 1967.

Lewy, Juilius. "Studies in Akkadian Grammar and Onomatology," *Orientalia*, N.S. 15 (1936), 361-415.

________. "Ḫatta, Ḫattu, Ḫatti, Ḫattuša and 'Old Assyrian' Ḫattum," *Archiv Orientální*, 18/3 (1950), 366-411.

________. "On Some Institutions of the Old Assyrian Empire," *Hebrew Union College Annual*, 27 (1956), 1-79.

Lods, Adolphe. "Une tablette inédite de Mari, intéressante pour l'histoire du prophétisme sémitique," in H. H. Rowley, ed., *Studies in Old Testament Prophecy Presented to Professor Theodore H. Robinson*, pp. 103-10. Edinburgh, 1950.

Marzal, A. "The Provincial Governor at Mari: His Title and Appointment" *Journal of Near Eastern Studies*, 30 (1971), 186-217.

________. "Two Officials Assisting the Provincial Governor at Mari," *Orientalia* 41 (1972), 359-77.

Moran, William L. "Akkadian Letters," in James B. Pritchard, ed., *Ancient Near Eastern Texts Relating to the Old Testament,* Third edition with Supplement, pp. 623-32. Princeton, 1969.

________. "New Evidence from Mari on the History of Prophecy," *Biblica*, 50 (1969), 15-56.

Munn-Rankin, J. M. "Diplomacy in Western Asia in the Early Second Millennium B.C.," *Iraq*, 18 (1956), 68-110.

Oppenheim, A. Leo. "The Archives of the Palace of Mari: A Review Article," *Journal of Near Eastern Studies*, 11 (1952), 129-39.

Page, Stephanie. "The Tablets from Tell Al-Rimah 1967: A Preliminary Report," *Iraq*, 30 (1968), 87-97.

________. "Ice, offerings and deities in the Old Babylonian texts from Tell el-Rimah," in *Actes de la XVIIe Rencontre Assyriologique Internationale* (Université Libre de Bruxelles, 30 juin-4 juillet 1969), pp. 181-83. Comité Belge de Recherches en Mésopotamie, 1970.

Powell, Marvin A., Jr. "A Note on the 'imērum' Measure at Mari," *Revue d'assyriologie et d'archéologie orientale*, 67 (1973), 77-78.

Reiner, Erica. "Fortune-Telling in Mesopotamia," *Journal of Near Eastern Studies*," 19 (1960), 23-35.

Renger, J. "Götternamen in der altbabylonischen Zeit," in *Heidelberger Studien zum alten Orient*, pp. 137-71. Wiesbaden, 1967.

________. "Untersuchungen zum Priestertum in der altbabylonischen Zeit, 1. Teil," *Zeitschrift für Assyriologie und verwandte Gebiete*, 58/N.F.

24 (1967), 110-88.

________. "Untersuchungen zum Priestertum in der altbabylonischen Zeit, 2 Teil," *Zeitschrift für Assyriologie und verwandte Gebiete*, 59/N.F. 25 (1969), 104-230.

Roberts, J. J. M. "The Hand of Yahweh," *Vetus Testamentum*, 21 (1971), 244-51.

Rosengarten, Yvonne. "La civilisation sumérienne de Lagash au milieu du IIIe millénaire, I," *Revue philosophique de la France et de l'étranger*, 155 (1965), 401-26.

Rouault, Oliver. "Andariq et Atamrum," *Revue d'assyriologie et d'archéologie orientale*, 64 (1970), 107-18.

Rowton, M. B. "Urban Autonomy in a Nomadic Environment," *Journal of Near Eastern Studies*, 32 (1973), 201-15.

________. "Autonomy and Nomadism in Western Asia," *Orientalia* 42 (1973), 247-58.

Sasson, Jack M. "Some Comments on Archive Keeping at Mari," *Iraq*, 34 (1972), 55-67.

________. "Biographical Notices on Some Royal Ladies from Mari," *Journal of Cuneiform Studies*, 25 (1973), 59-78.

Scharbert, Josef. "'Fluchen' und 'Segnen' im Alten Testament," *Biblica*, 39 (1958), 1-26.

Sjöberg, Åke W. "Zu einigen Verwandtschaftsbezeichnungen in Sumerischen," in *Heidelberger Studien zum alten Orient*, pp. 201-31. Wiesbaden, 1967.

Soden, Wolfram von. "Zu den politischen Korrespondenzen des Archivs von Mâri," *Orientalia*, N.S. 21 (1952), 75-86.

________. "Neue Bände der Archives Royales de Mâri," *Orientalia*, N.S. 22 (1953), 193-209.

________. "Gebet II," in *Reallexikon der Assyriologie*, Band III, pp. 160-70. Berlin, 1957-.

________. "Die Schutzgenien lamassu und schudu in der babylonisch-assyrischen Literature," *Baghdader Mitteilungen*, 3 (1964), 148-56.

________. "Einige Bemerkungen zu den von Fr. Ellermeier in 'Prophetie in Mari und Israel' (Herzberg 1968), Erstmalig bearbeiteten Briefen aus ARM 10," *Ugarit-Forschungen*, 1 (1969), 198-99.

Thureau-Dangin, François. "Iaḫadunlim, roi de Ḫana," *Revue d'assyriologie et d'archéologie orientale*, 33 (1936), 49-54.

Ungnad, Arthur. "Datenlisten," in *Reallexikon der Assyriologie*, Band II, pp. 131-94. Berlin and Leipzig, 1938.

Vaux, Roland de. "Sur le voile des femmes dans l'Orient ancien," *Revue biblique*, 44 (1935), 397-412. (Reprinted in *Bible et Orient*, pp. 407-23. Paris, 1967.)

Weider, Ernst. "Hof- und Harems-Erlasse assyrischer Könige," *Archiv für Orientforschung*, 17/2 (1956), 257-93.

Book Reviews

Falkenstein, Adam. Review of *Archives royales de Mari, I*, by Georges Dossin, *Archives royales de Mari, II*, by Ch. F. Jean, and *Archives royales de Mari, III*, by J.-R. Kupper, in *Bibliotheca Orientalis*, 11 (1954), 112-17.

Harris, Rivkah. Review of *Histoire mondiale de la femme. Préhistoire et antiquité*, sous la direction de Pierre Grimal, in *Journal of the Economic and Social History of the Orient*, 9 (1966), 308-9.

________. Review of *Cuneiform Texts from Babylonian Tablets in the British Museum, Part XLVIII: Legal Documents*, copied by J. J. Finkelstein, in *Journal of the Economic and Social History of the Orient*, 13 (1970), 315-18.

Hirsch, Hans. Review of *Archives royales de Mari, IX: Textes administratifs de la salle 5*, by Maurice Birot, in *Zeitschrift für Assyriologie und verwandte Gebiete*, 56/N.F. 22 (1964), 282-84.

Sasson, Jack M. Review of *Frauenbriefe uber Religion, Politik und Privatleben in Mari*, by Wm. H. Ph. Römer, in *Bibliotheca Orientalis*, 28 (1971), 354-56.

________. Review of *Actes de la XVIIe Rencontre Assyriologique Internationale*, edited by André Finet, in *Journal of Near Eastern Studies*, 32 (1973), 340-41.

Veenhoff, K. R. Review of *Baghdader Mitteilungen*, Band 3 (1964): *Festschrift für Ernst Heinrich zum 65. Geburtstag am 15. Dezember 1965*, in *Bibliotheca Orientalis*, XXV (1968), 195-98.

INDEXES

I. Mari Texts Treated or Cited

ARM III 40 121
41.13-16 19
42 79-80, 89(7)
42.10-11 19
45.15-21 17
63.4-12 35(87)
63.8-9 19
63-64 24
64 35(87)
78 121
84 79-81, 89(7)
84.6 19
84.11-12 86
84.21f. 90(17)
84.24 19
84.26-27 80, 90(16)

IV 24.20-23 57(44)
59.5f. 133(1)
72.31f. 89(9)

V 16.11-13 133(18)
25.5, 15 133(1)
46.8-11 132
65.30f. 133(1)
75.12′ 133(1)
79 89(10)
82 96
82.19 103(2)

VI 15 12(b)
18 12(b)
26 52, 63
27.13′ 104(20)
30.29 133(1)
38.13′ 75(32)
39 34(62)

ARM VI 39.24-25 32(41)
40 34(62)
45 19, 121, 122
46 90(21)
46.4 85
67.7 19
73 89(10)
74 17, 133(1)
75 19
76.20 137

VII 13.8 104(27)
48 51
91.5 139(3)
105 75(27)
123.12-13 139(3)
125 42, 139(3)
130.2 55(16)
139.1 87
139.1-2 92(44)
155 70(40)
180.iii.7′ 34(74)
199.22′ 57(45)
203.1 42, 139(3)
203.7′ 139(3)
206 23
206.6 115
206.8 26
206.10 22
206.4′ 86
206.4′-5′ 92(44)
206.r.7′ 21
206.r.8′-9′ 23
206.r.9′ 62
206.r.10′ 57(48), 58(56)
217.3 34(68)
220.1 86

II. <u>Names of Deities</u>

Ištara-danna 128
Itur-Mer 23, 66, 75(28), 126(12), 130-31
Lagamal 18
Nanna 30(2)
Tešub 131
Ninurta 105(36)
Šamaš 51, 93-98, 102, 103(17), 104(19, 21-22, 27), 105(36), 119, 121, 129-31

III. Personal Names

Abdu-šuri 62
Abi-esuḫ 103(5)
Adalšeni 117(8)
Addu-duri 11-12, 19, 33(60), 57(39), 59, 64-73, 75(27, 30, 33, 36), 113(5), 123-24, 127(16), 128, 136
Admubalaṭi 139(3)
Aḫatum 35(95), 50, 121-23, 126(14)
Aḫum 19, 66-67, 75(22), 122, 126(9)
Akatiya 34(68)
Ama-dugga 59, 72-73, 76(37), 136
Ammiditana 105(32)
Aškur-Addu 53, 63-64
Atamrum 50
Atta-ili-ma 24
Attùkki 130, 133(16)
Awat-Aya 103(16)
Aya-arri 107(59)
Ayalatum 103(5)
Azzu- 62-63
Baḫdi-Lim 11-13, 17, 19, 33(62), 52, 59
Baḫlatum 92(44)
Balumenuḫḫe 72
Baranamtara 8
Belassunu 23, 58(61), 59, 61-64, 73
Belet- 139(3)
Bunuma-Addu 14
Buqaqum (Puqaqum) 16, 33(51)
Dadi-Ḫadun 9, 31(11), 131
Dagan-malik 35(95), 121, 123, 126(14)
Dam-ḫurasi 11-12, 21-23, 25, 34(74)
Dan(?)-na-na 121, 127(15)
Dariš-libur 15, 57(40)
Duḫšatum 50
Eli-eressa 103(16)
Enḫeduanna 30(2)
Erišti-Aya 25, 30(7), 37, 50, 54(1), 93-107, 129
Ermi-Addu 96
Gabiatum 130
Gašera (Kašerum) 31(10)
Gimiliya 103(16)
Ḫabdu-malik 55(16)
Ḫali-Ḫadun 15-16
Ḫammurapi 9, 103(5), 114, 116
Ḫamu-šagiš 64
Ḫaqba-Ḫammu (Aqba-ḫammu) 62-64, 74(16)
Ḫatni-Addu 9, 71-72, 75(34)
Ḫatni-El (Ḫadni-El, Ḫatni-iluma) 71, 75(32)
Ḫaya-abum 33(55)

IV. Geographical Names

Babylon 95, 99, 103(5, 16-17), 105(32), 114, 137
Baliḫ 15
Burundum 117(8)
Cappadocia 74(9)
Dilbat 103(16)
Dir 68
DUMU(.MEŠ) sim'āl 111, 113(4)
Dunnum 44, 56(26)
Dur-Yaḫdun-Lim 21, 67
Ebabbar 94-95, 103(17), 104(19)
Edikukalamma (Esakudkalamma) 103(17)
Egirzalanki 95, 104(18)
Eluḫut 40
Emutbalum 114, 117(5)
Ešnunna 16, 60
Ḫalab, *see* Aleppo
Ḫalabit 57(51)
Ḫana 44, 137
Ḫišamta 18, 33(59)
Idamaraz 42, 52, 56(25)
Ilanṣura 42, 44-45, 48, 50, 52, 55(18), 56(29), 136
Ilum-muluk 56(26)
Israel 25, 30(8)
Kallassu 118(10), 119-21, 126(6)
Karana 33(52), 53, 58(61), 61-64
Kirdaḫat 56(25)
Kish 8
Kulmiš 79, 81-85, 87, 90(20, 22), 109
Kurda 33(52), 67
Lagash 8, 103(17), 104(19)
Larsa 103(8, 17), 104(19)
Mari 3 *et passim*
Nahur 15-16, 37, 40-41, 54(6), 55(13)
Nippur 105(36), 134(19)
Qatanum 71
Qaṭara 62
Qatna 20, 34(81), 52, 129, 131
Qattunan 12, 21, 64
Sagaratum 21, 128
Sippar 50, 93-95, 98-100, 102 103(5, 16-17), 104(21-22, 27), 105(34, 36), 119, 121
Sumer 137
Ṣubatum 68
Šakka 123
Šubat-Enlil 51
Šuna 48-49, 52, 57(46)
Terqa 12, 15, 17-19, 21-25, 60-61, 75(27), 79-81, 86-87, 89, 90(20), 104(21-22), 113(8), 119-23, 128-30
Tigris 64
Tizraḫ 55(16), 118(10)
Tuttul 119-21
Turukkū 52
Ugarit 30(8)
Ur 30(2), 103(8)
Uruk 103(8), 117
Yamḫad 9, 31(12), 52
Yapturum 37
Yariḫ 16
Zabalum 55(16)
Ziniyan 68